Segway Into My New Life

A Story of Diagnosis

By Meg Lewellyn

Comments & Praise

"I want to be you. You never quit the journey and I am so proud of you and what you have accomplished. People write books about this and make tons of money and you just shared a TRUE, REAL LIFE story that became. I pray that you continue on this path and remain true to yourself, for you deserve every little microscopic minute of it!"

"Really great blog. You are truly an inspiration! I hope your story touches many people."

"So cool to read these because it makes me feel that I'm not alone."

"Thank you for sharing so openly and with humor."

"Thank you so much for sharing your story! It has been almost 5 months since my first "flare" and my neurologist says this will pass quickly… one day, I will wake up and be perfectly fine again—yeah, well I had to use a cane yesterday for a shopping trip with my family (huge issue for me). It is encouraging to know that there are others that don't follow whatever the textbook path this disease takes—is there a textbook for this? You make me laugh and I thank you so much for that!"

"Your stories make me smile because they are real like mine… I was also diagnosed in 2011. I am trying to figure this thing out and it is so nice to read about your journey and to know that it does suck sometimes. I started medical MJ too this year. I can't believe how clear my head is! Thank you for your humor and honesty."

"Thank you so much for giving a voice to something that most people find difficult to talk about! I have spina bifida and my lesion for that has given me the same fun problems your MS has. It's nice to see someone like me who finds the humor in any situation."

"Superb, had me laughing all night..."

"I have to say I was LOL'ing my way through your evening. But it IS because I can and because I love you too much not to!"

"Yet another one of your stories that makes me laugh so hard I'm afraid I might wet MY pants! Thank goodness you DO have such a good sense of humor."

"I found your "life reporting" to be very interesting and I commend you for your positive attitude toward living fully. You have been dealt a tough hand to play and you are doing a great job of handling it! Very few kids worldwide are fortunate to have a CAMP MOMMA to lead them through life."

"... keep telling your story Meg and people will listen. You'll be amazed how many people will stumble across your blog in the middle of the night, and read something that makes a difference to them or someone they know."

"Oh, ughhh. Sorry to hear about that. Somehow, you convey such a crappy situation in a very entertaining way, though."

"I was looking at around at many blogs and yours "spoke" to me because of your honesty and humor. I felt as if you were writing from your heart and just really being you. You're a natural."

"... I really enjoy reading your blog because it shows me that I am not the only one in this universe, there is a nice person on the other side of the world, dealing with the same problems. Thanks for your blog, Meg!"

"... Just thanks for posting this and the pictures, made me feel less embarrassed and made me a laugh a bit."

"Meg this is some of the funniest shit I've read in a while. Keep up the great blog!!"

"I am laughing so hard after this because I have been in this exact situation."

"Thank you for sharing this! Love your sense of humor!"

"This is what makes you so great; someone somewhere will NEED to read this, because it will happen to them. Well done for writing it and for laughing so soon."

"OK, I am in work reading this, laughing my fool ass off (and making my coworkers wonder what's so funny about being in work on a Friday). You, my dear, are what it is all about. The humor and the honesty is SOOOOO refreshing! We all have to laugh to get through life! You have written what I only have pictured in my mind. Thank you for this wonderful post and for your sense of humor!"

"Thank you so much for being honest and real with your post. I can relate to a lot of your stories and it's great to know that I am not alone!!!!"

"Wow! What a journey! Hats off to you girl! Inspirational..."

"Thank you for being so very brave, dilligent and for thriving to be the best!"

"It's like you're in my head; living with MS has forced me to decide what REALLY matters; to constantly ask the question "is this worth my time and energy?"

"Thank you for showing me that I am not alone."

Segway Into My New Life

A Story of Diagnosis

By Meg Lewellyn

ISBN-13: 978-1727874235
ISBN-10: 1727874234

Editing by Jessica Loving-Campos
Cover artwork by Jessica Leigh Hernandez
www.jessicaleighhernandez.com
Biography photo by Piper A. Shethar

Printed in the United States of America
First Printing, 2018

Published by Meg Lewellyn
www.bbhwithms.com

This book captures one woman's journey through MS diagnosis and does not in any way make any medical claims that should be taken over the advice of a medical professional.

Thank You

I would like to thank all of the friends and family that were there for me during my early years with this disease, for always supporting me and encouraging me on my crazy quest to remain "normal."

I would like to thank the old high-school friend who became my "oh shit" person. He was the person that I would reach out to when things got really bad and I didn't think I could keep moving forward. I shared with him when I couldn't look others in the eye. I shared my deepest and darkest fears. Each chapter begins with a piece of sage advice this friend offered and I am forever grateful for his kindness and humor.

To all the MSers and others on social media with whom I have connected over the years through my blog and various online support groups: Thank you for your words of kindness, support and encouragement. It's because of you that I have kept writing and I am finally seeing this book get published!

To my kids: thank you for always being there with me on this journey (not that you had much of a choice). Thank you for being amazing and awesome and for understanding that your mom isn't "normal" and being OK with that.

To my parents: thank you for always loving me and for putting up with my stubborness and need to try and do things "my way." Knowing that I have always had your support has made this journey a lot easier.

To Shawn, believe it or not, I don't have enough words to express how much you mean to me and how grateful I am that we found each other. If other people are actually reading this, then that means I actually published this book and I have you to thank for that. You make me believe in myself again!

And last but not least, I would be remiss to not mention my "Poker Playing" doctor. Although I have not had contact with him in years, he played such a huge role in shaping how I viewed my diagnosis and how I have approached this journey.

After all, this is not an "oh fuck" moment.

Contents

Chapter One
I've Fallen and I Can't Get Up

"I am sorry to hear about your situation. I cannot tell you I know what you are feeling, but, I can tell you, you will get through it. You are strong and you are going to be OK."

It's a cold, wet Monday and as I maneuver "Bessy the Bus"—my silver, sticker-laden VW Eurovan into a space in the parking lot of Target, my mind wanders. Four days ago I had a spinal tap. This morning, I returned to the hospital for a spinal patch and now I am sitting in my car, listening as the rain pummels the roof, thinking that I am teetering on losing it. I'm just seconds away from having a complete and nuclear meltdown.

After extracting my spinal fluid with a big ass needle, it was shipped off to be analyzed by some random lab technician at the Mayo Clinic. As I see it, my future now lies in their hands. I wonder if he or she knows. I wonder if they ever think of the living, breathing human being that provided the specimen that they are examining, or is my fluid seen as just another vial in a day full of vials?

It is the not knowing that is killing me. This thing, whatever it is that is "wrong" with me, has taken over my every waking thought and it is doing a damn good job of keeping me up at night too. My thoughts are all over the place. One minute, I think that I will be OK; that no

1

matter what the results show, I will be strong enough to handle whatever it is that they tell me. But then seconds later, thoughts of cancer and dying slip in and I begin to panic again. I can't leave my kids. Their mom can't die. That is not how the story is supposed to go…

I shake my head as I reach for my rain jacket and open the driver's door to the onslaught of rain. I know that I need to stop obsessing about all of this. I know that I will drive myself absolutely bat shit crazy if I don't stop with the mind games of "what if…" The good news is that I have plenty of things to do to keep my mind off of the stress of waiting, of the not knowing. Turkey Day is coming and I have a shit ton to do to prepare to be the hostess with the mostest.

Traditionally, the holiday has been spent at our house, with a variety of family and friends joining us. Although I am no Martha Stewart, I enjoy cooking and preparing the house for these special occasions. I put 100% into such endeavors, and always try to top what I have done in the past.

Given my current physical condition and all that I have been through recently with doctor appointments, MRIs, and the aforementioned spinal tap, my family and friends expressed concern when I announced that we will still have the festivities at our house. My parents (being three thousand miles away) posed the strongest opposition to this. I had promised them that I would go easy. I swore that I would get the turkey prepared and cooked from our local market. I promised that I would make mashed potatoes from a box and I had even said that I would pick up store made pies. All things I would never have considered on any other year but am now promising because I need to host this holiday, I need to try and pretend to be "normal." I need to be OK.

I lied! I didn't intend to, but I just can't follow through with my promises! I need to do the things that I have always done. I need to forget about all of my fears. I need to leave the tears behind and be with family and friends. We have nine people coming (making the total number fourteen) and even though most are family (my husband's cousins and mother, along with my brother and sister-in-law), I don't want to let them know that I am struggling or to concede that this thing is getting to me. After all, it is a temporary illness and I will get better. That's what the doctor said at my appointment last week, before the first MRI, before baring my ass as he stuck the needle into my spine. So why complain about it, or let it change my life in any way?

After my stop at Target on Monday, I kick preparations into high-gear on Tuesday with a trip to the grocery store and Trader Joe's. Wednesday, I spend cleaning and decorating and I stay up chatting, chopping and cooking with my sister-in-law and brother after they arrive from Portland. I wake on Thanksgiving morning only hours after I had said my "goodnights" and as I lower my feet to the carpet, I can already tell that my legs are not very happy with my recent activities. But I don't have time to coddle them. I have a party that must go on.

The candles are shimmering from all areas of our great room which includes our kitchen, dining room, living room and the kids' TV area. The fire, built to ward off the day's rain and dampness, is snapping and crackling, filling the room with a warmth that is more than just temperature-based. The table has been set and includes a beautiful Jacquard tablecloth in autumnal hues, linen napkins tied with organza ribbons, classic bone white china, wine goblets that sparkle in the candle light, and the center of the table is lined with a mixture of candles, fresh fruit, and pumpkins decorated by the kids.

I have managed to convince them to change out of their torn jeans and stained t-shirts into "nicer" clothes (meaning at least clean). Although for Piper, a request is not needed, as she has eagerly anticipated the occasion to wear her new maroon and black velvet holiday dress. The scene is one of warmth and happiness, and as I take one last glance before heading up to change, I am pleased with the results of my labor.

The stress of the past month has not agreed with me or my appetite and as a result, I have dropped about eight pounds, which I really don't have to spare; leaving me thinner than I should or want to be. As I stand in my closet, I notice that my legs and feet are feeling heavy and tired. I glance at the bed and wonder if there is time for me to lie down, time for me to take a little rest before the our guests arrive. I have never been a big fan of naps, but lately I have been exhausted and I seem to think about napping a hell of a lot.

I am still contemplating a quick visit with my bed, when I hear the doorbell. So much for naptime. I open the closet door and quickly grab a black and white print wrap dress that is one of my standard "go-to" dresses. Usually form fitting, it now hangs loosely from my body, accentuating my unhealthy size and figure. I zip up my black boots, run a brush through my hair, and apply a quick coat of lip-gloss before I head back downstairs to greet our guests.

My mother-in-law is the first to arrive and once I take her coat, she gives me the perfunctory kiss on my cheek, leaving a nearly un-re-movable coral lipstick stain. She immediately exclaims, "Megan, you look wonderful!"

Having feared that everyone would notice and obsess over the fact that I am not looking well, I graciously accept this compliment, while I think to myself, "she's trying to make me feel good? That's a new one, but appreciated."

The afternoon is filled with great conversation, wonderful wine and fun and games. We have a giant Scrabble board inlaid in the pavers of our front courtyard and since my brother and sister-in-law are avid Scrabblers, and it isn't raining (unusual for Seattle), a group head out for a heated game of words and wisdom. The kids join in, ensuring that the mixture of words are amusing, to say the least.

The turkey falls off the bone, the garlic mashed potatoes, sweet cur-ried carrots, orange cranberry chutney with pecans, braised brussels sprouts, caesar salad, and homemade rolls are eagerly gobbled up by all in attendance, with profuse praise being showered on me. Once I have served up the pies (not store-bought as I promised, but made and brought by others, at least), I refill wine glasses for those that need a top-off, and brew a pot of coffee.

I, then, set to work on cleaning the kitchen. My mother-in-law and daughter are sitting at the island that faces the sink. Up until this point in the day, I have had very little interaction with my mother-in-law, which is probably a good thing. She isn't always a nice person, and I often find myself stressed out when I am in her company.

But at the moment, she has me as a captive audience and decides to regale me (and Piper) on some of her views. She starts by again saying how good I look. I again thank her for the compliment. She then says, "You are so skinny!" I am beginning to rethink my assessment of her earlier compliment at the door. I had chocked it up to her trying to make me feel good but I am beginning to suspect that how I feel has little to do with her words.

I reply, "Alin, I am too skinny, I am not well, and as a result have lost weight that I didn't need to lose."

Her response is, "but you look so good, and you are so skinny!"

What the fuck? Again with the skinny? Piper, looking beautiful in her party dress, has been sitting there during this exchange, just quietly listening, taking it all in. She is seven and has already begun to express unhappiness with her own body image saying, "Mom, I'm fat" or grabbing her stomach saying, "look at all this fat." I vividly remember how difficult it was to be a young girl and being "big boned." I remember not liking my body. I work very hard at trying to help Piper with this. I want her to love herself and her body irrelevant of its size. Yet here is her grandmother, repeatedly complimenting her own mom on her "skinniness." As I turn to the sink to begin scrubbing the pots and pans that have been soaking, I hear my mother-in-law address my daughter directly, "Piper, always remember, a woman can never be too skinny."

My immediate reaction is to turn to her and scream, "shut the fuck up!" Fortunately for me, the filter seems to be working today. I think it, but don't say a word. I remember that my impressionable daughter is right here, and that we have a house full of people enjoying a lovely holiday I have worked hard to put together. So instead, of ripping my mother-in-law's head off, I quietly ask Piper to go and see if anyone wants any more wine or coffee (to get her away from this toxic woman). I, then gather up the trash bag from the kitchen can and head to the garage to take it to the bin out on the street.

I'd like to think that I storm out but really at this point, I hobble out. My legs are exhausted. I have barely sat for a moment since the alarm so rudely woke me at 5:30 a.m. Based on the past few months and what I have experienced, I know that I am pushing their limits with every minute that I remain upright. I notice that it has begun to rain and think for a second of turning back to grab my rain jacket hanging on the hook just inside the kitchen door, but I know that even laying eyes on my mother-in-law again may set me off, and decide against the jacket. As I struggle with the overstuffed bag of turkey bones and food scraps, my mind is reeling.

How dare she! How could someone that is a grandmother be so insensitive to the things she is saying and their impact on young ears? But then, I remember exactly who I am talking about, and realize, of course she would; without ever giving it a thought or even seeing it as inappropriate. After twelve years of marriage, I have learned that this is who she is and what she does, and that is not going to change. I have worked hard over the years to keep the peace with her and encourage her to be a part of our children's lives, but I also will do anything in my power to protect them from her manipulative and often cruel behavior.

I lug the bag into the open bin, brush off my hands and stand for a moment, thinking, "I really don't want to go back in there." I slowly begin my way back up the driveway, when something shiny catches my eye in the courtyard. Someone has left a glass of wine on the table after wrapping up the game of Scrabble. This is a task I can do to stall just a bit longer. I can grab the glass and then just make sure everything else out here is cleaned up and put away. I am getting pretty wet, but it seems to beat the hell out of going back in and seeing her.

As I stumble around the courtyard, looking for other forgotten items, my mind is in overdrive. I keep thinking, "you don't need this, you can't handle this right now. You are sick, and you need to focus on you and getting better and not what your crazy ass mother-in-law might say or do." I flash back to all that I have been through in the past few months, the MRI, the spinal tap, the spinal patch, and all the pain, frustration and fear I have felt. Why can't this woman, for once, just come to a family gathering and not stir up trouble? Why does she do and say the things that she does?

As I finish my round of the area, I grab the half full goblet of wine and turn to head back through the garage and into the house and whatever is waiting there for me. My foot hits an uneven paver and I trip. The goblet of wine goes up as I go down. Hard. I don't manage to get my hands out in time to break the fall. Just after I hit the ground, the goblet and wine follow the rules of gravity and find their way down to me and shatter upon impact.

I'm lying in the pouring rain, covered in shattered glass, wine and blood; unable to get up because my legs have gone paralyzed and all I can do is laugh. As hard as I try, I cannot get back up. I think of the old TV ad, with the elderly woman in the bathroom, that uses her alert button to announce, "help, I've fallen and I can't get up!" Where is my damn button? I fall into another fit of laughter and giggles. I realize that no one knows where I am, or even that I am missing, and wonder how long it will be before someone notices my absence and comes looking for me. Will they think to look outside?

I lie there, unable to move my legs at all. I lie back and feel the rain hit my face, knowing my tears from laughing are becoming indistinguishable from the rain as both run down my cheeks. Suddenly I find something else to laugh about. What if my neighbors see me like this? Holy shit, talk about the rumor mill! They will all think I have really tied one on for the holiday—gone and gotten drunk off my ass! I am out in the rain, laughing to myself like a madwoman and time just ticks on. The party is still going, my guests are inside, soaking up the warmth and coziness I created for them while I lie here, soaking up the rain.

I'm not sure how long I have been lying out here. I don't know how much time has elapsed since the goblet went up and I went down, but eventually one of the kids sees me, outside, on the ground, in the rain, covered in shards of glass and red merlot. I'm not sure which of these conditions clued them into the fact that there "might be a problem with mom," but they seem to put it together fairly quickly and run to find their father.

My husband arrives at the door and without a word, picks me up and carries me into the house, straight up the stairs to our bedroom. I don't know it then, but I won't see any of my guests again tonight, I won't be at the door saying the final goodbyes and checking to make sure everyone has remembered their dishes and leftovers. I will also not have to participate in any of the clean-up. Note to self: an excellent way to have the kitchen cleaned by someone else—fall down and lie in the pouring rain for a bit. It may be small but I'll take any perks I can get when it comes to whatever medical bullshit I am currently going through.

Once I am up in our bedroom, he begins to wrestle me out of my rain, blood, and wine soaked clothes. I'm not much help. I still cannot move either of my legs and can no longer feel them at all. As I lay motionless in an attempt to make his quest to undress me easier, it strikes me that he seems so angry. I can understand that he is concerned, hell I am concerned, but I don't understand why he would be mad at me. I didn't try to fall, I didn't choose to hang out in the rain. I feel like I have no control over what my body is doing and it makes me incredibly sad that he seems to be blaming me for whatever the hell is wrong with me. It crosses my mind that maybe this would be a good time to talk about everything that has been going on over the past few months. To open up to him about how nervous and scared I am.

But the minute I try and bring up the subject, he tells me that this is not the time or the place to be talking about "such" things. He reminds me that we have a house full of guests and after plopping another blanket on top of my dead legs, he turns to leave. Just as he is about to walk out of the room, I realize that I am famished! Given that I have had no appetite for weeks this revelation is huge! I quickly ask him to get me something to eat.

Twenty minutes later, he returns and hands me a Cliff bar. As I hold it in my hand and turn it over to see what flavor he has selected for me, I feel the tears well up in my eyes. I have just spent the better part of my week preparing a feast fit for a king. There is enough food downstairs to feed an army! Good food! I should know, I made it. Yet, he couldn't be bothered to bring me more than this lame ass protein bar.

I try and express this to him and his reply is, "you know that you will probably only eat a few bites, and this small bar is packed with the nutrition and protein you need." Quite an endorsement for Cliff bars, but again, not what I am craving!

Really? Now he is going to express concern for my health? For my well being? Where the fuck was this concern last week when I drove myself to the hospital to get the spinal tap? Where was he for the hours that I lay in the MRI tube, freaking out that I might be dying. This stupid bar seems to sum up our relationship, our marriage. It is going to leave me feeling empty and wanting more.

He leaves to see to our guests and the clean-up I have so skillfully avoided. Minutes later, Piper slips into the room and asks if I want her to go down and get me a plate full of food. I don't even hesitate, "Yes, please!"

She returns and is precariously holding a tray, on which sits not only a plate piled high with all the dishes I have made, but a small vase with a single flower from the centerpiece arrangement and I find myself crying again. My emotions seem to being running wild, and I try to hide my tears from her as she lays the tray on the bed next to my still "dead" legs.

Just as I am about to dig in, she asks if I will wait a minute for her and she slips out of the room again. I sit on the bed, listening to my stomach growl as I make swirls and peaks in my mashed potatoes and wonder where she's gone. She is an amazing little girl, with so much spirit and heart, and I wonder what she thinks of all that has been going on with me lately. The trips to the doctors, the whispered phone calls to my parents late at night, finding me lying in the pouring rain. I don't understand it, and I am the one living it, so I can't imagine what she thinks of all of this.

I quickly swipe at the tears when I hear her coming down the hallway and burst out laughing when she enters the room. She has returned with a huge ass bowl of mashed potatoes, the dish that her grandmother told her she shouldn't eat at dinner. She has changed into her pajamas and now joins me in bed. We curl up with our food and I click on the TV and find a movie to watch. I don't pay much attention to the movie, because it really doesn't matter. I am snuggled up with my little girl, sharing a moment that I doubt I will ever forget.

The past few months have been scary as shit. I don't know what is wrong with me, I don't know whether the doctor is right and everything will turn out fine, or if it something more, something that will forever change me and my life. But right here, right now, everything is alright, everything is perfect, because I have my little people with me. They are my everything. They constantly fill my heart with wonder and awe and fill my life with happiness and love. I know that no matter what happens down the road, we are going to be in this together and things will be OK.

Chapter Two

Mother's Helper

"Sometimes even the strong ones ask for help.
It usually makes us stronger."

I suppose I should take a step or two back and tell you a little about myself before I continue to share my journey. The essentials are: I turned thirty-seven last month, I have been married for eleven years and we have three young children (Sam is nine, Piper is seven and Maxon "Macky" turned five this year.) I lead a very active life; I run 6-8 miles almost every day, I hit the gym for strength and core training daily, I swim a lot inside or out throughout the year, and chasing three little ones keeps me on my toes and going at full-speed all day, every day.

I don't remember much about who I was before I had my children, but I don't say this in some forlorn, longing way. You can't miss something that you don't remember and to be honest, I don't spend time thinking about the "before" because I love who I am now. I am a momma. It's what I do, it's what I love. It is what I was meant to be.

Sure, I had hopes and dreams of other seemingly grander things. My six-year-old heart knew that I was meant to be either a lifeguard or a figure skater. By the end of high school, I headed off to college with every intention of becoming either a social worker or a special needs teacher. But even as a young girl, I loved babies and children.

I remember, at the ripe age of ten, running up the sidewalk, beneath the canopy of leaves from the great oak trees that lined the streets of the upper-middle class Connecticut neighborhood where I grew up. I would stand on the front porch of the McDonald's house, amidst the piles of shoes, roller-skates and hockey sticks, waiting for Sam, their blue eyed, tow-headed toddler, or their moppy dog, Mac, to hear my arrival. I would feel overwhelmed with excitement to see the shaggy heads of a boy and his dog peek around the corner of the stairs, to hear his giggles and squeals.

This was my very first job. My official title was "Mother's Helper." My job description included tasks, such as:
1. Play with Sam
2. Give Sam & Mac snacks
3. Play with Sam & Mac in the backyard
4. Take Sam & Mac for a walk

Let me just say, I nailed it! I was the best little "Mother's Helper" to ever darken the doorsteps of Connecticut back in 1980! I remember standing in the doorway as Sam's mom bounced him on one hip, while holding the screen door with the other. The silver bracelets that always adorned her wrists jingled as she reached into the pocket of her cut-off shorts and handed me my hard-earned dollar. She was the first mom (other than my own mother) that made me think, I want to grow up to be just like her. Standing on that porch, those hours spent with a little boy and his dog were my first tinglings of motherhood.

The point is that I love kids; I always have. So when I found myself married at the age of twenty-five to a man nine years my senior, I fully embraced and endorsed the topic of starting a family and having babies. Sam arrived June 4th, 1998 and from that moment on, "who" I was took on a whole new meaning and definition. I was now a mother, I/ we had created our very own tiny, little person. A little man who would grow and learn and become a big man, but would still be mine—he would always be a part of me going forward. Something I made!

Nothing before that moment could ever compare to how that felt, to know that this living being was going to depend on me. To realize that my purpose was now to provide for and protect him, to guide him in the right directions and steer him clear of danger and disasters was an amazing feeling. All the love and joy that I had felt for other people's children seemed so inconsequential to what I felt for my own child. Knowing that I would be able to shower him with love and joy and share in his growing into an actual real person was both overwhelming and calming at the same time. Overwhelming because raising a child, making a good person is no small task and shooting this little guy out of my vagina had signed me up for a long ass journey as a mom. But it was also calming, because it was the moment that something I had always dreamed of being came to fruition. I was someone's mommy.

I loved every minute of it. Sure, there were moments that were less than "picture perfect," like when my eighteen-month-old "bundle of joy" decided to rip his diaper off and finger paint the walls of his room with his own shit. That wasn't a blissful mommy moment. Neither was when I walked the steep hills of our Seattle neighborhood in the misty rain for an entire night. From 10 p.m. until 5:30 a.m., I trekked up and down those damn hills hoping to ward off the fits of croup that had threatened to close off my little boy's airway. There was no bliss in that night. But at the end of day, it was what I was meant to be—I had gotten the best job ever—someone to care for, forever.

Piper arrived two years later (well, actually two years and four days if you want to get technical) and Sam loved his little sister, for the most part. Knowing that for the first time, he was going to have to share me with another little being, I decided that it would be a good idea to try and slowly warm him to the idea of having a baby join our family. Much to the dismay and horror of my husband, I headed off to our local Goodwill and picked up a little baby doll and a small toy baby stroller. I thought that giving my almost two-year-old son a baby of his own was a great way to prepare him for the impending arrival of baby number two.

And it actually worked... a little too well. After spending a few weeks hauling Sam's baby around with us on trips to the park, grocery store and even on a camping trip, he had become a great little daddy. Well versed in strapping it into the car seat (yes, I did bust out his old infant seat to get him used to the idea of two car seats, and he immediately decided that "his" baby had to be safe too), changing diapers and even "feeding" the baby a bottle, I thought to myself, my boy is going to make a great father someday.

Here is where I made a tactical mistake, a grave error that would lead to more than a few headaches and a few to many glasses of wine needed at the end of the day once I no longer had "my" baby in my belly. I didn't think to mention to Sam that the doll was just a temporary baby. Just a stand-in, a trial run to prepare him for his real baby, the baby in my belly.

So when Piper arrived, he was loving and gentle, and interested... in introducing his new sister to "his" baby. He was curious to see what mommy did with "her" baby, but had no intention of sharing "his" baby's things. That meant that the baby seat that I had already wrestled into a secure spot weeks before Piper arrived was apparently not where "my" baby was going to sit. That one was Sam's baby's car seat and I, of course, would need to get "my" baby her own car seat. Any thought of using the nice new expensive baby bottles I had purchased and then carefully washed and stored in the sippy cup drawer in the height of my nesting phase went right out the window. Those were "his" baby's bottles, not Piper's.

I found myself wondering what the hell I was doing with my life as I bundled Sam, Piper and "his" baby into the car and schlepped back to the highly over-priced children's store in the hoity-toity community that oftentimes reminds me of the places of my childhood; the small, quaint towns of New England.

I parked the car, and realized I was much too close to the large Hummer parked in the next spot and extracting the three kids (yes, three) would be a challenge. But it was raining and I hadn't seen any other spots as I crawled along the main street, past Starbucks and Sam's favorite ice cream shop. So I was left to try and squeeze my "still plump from childbirth" body out of the car, while desperately trying to not scratch or ding the stupid Hummer taking up a space and a half.

As the four of us tumbled into the shop, we took up just about every available inch of space, and almost immediately were standing in the puddles we created as we came in from the rain. I quickly recognized the packaging of the baby bottles that my research had assured me would be the best for my new baby and grabbed four, and turned to the white-haired, granny-looking woman behind the register.

Not surprisingly, she instantly went into the, "boy you have got your hands full" spiel. Even though "my" baby was only a few weeks old, I'd become quite accustomed to this type of small talk in the weeks before her arrival. When it was just me and Sam, my baby bump and "his" baby, people would say that. Rightfully so. I looked like I was a traveling circus of babies. So she was completely accurate in her assessment. Thanks to Sam's baby needing to come along, I did have my hands full and I had something wrong with me that she didn't even know about!

We had our moments, but for the most part, my two little sidekicks got along and loved spending time with eachother and me. When Maxon joined us two years later (this time I made it to July before popping him out), it just meant I had one more child to love and hang out with. I was happy. I'll say it again: being a mom is what I was meant to be.

Time flies; any parent can tell you that. Days of wrestling car seats, juggling bottles, sippy cups, and hauling dirty diapers around were quickly replaced with lunch boxes, backpacks, field trips, school concerts, and soccer practices. My little babies had turned into toddlers, and then morphed in young children.

But that really isn't the point of this diversion to the story. I am sharing this to explain how I found myself lying in the rain, paralyzed and laughing my ass off. I have painted a picture of my role as mom and I have expressed my love of my children but before I bounce ahead to six months ago when I first began to suspect that there was something wrong with me, I would be leaving quite a bit out of the picture to not mention my "better" half; the man whom I married and decided to procreate with.

In 1995, I met a man who was on a mission. His family history (a thing of great pride for him) revealed that no male had ever been older than the age of thirty-three when first getting married. Why this even remotely mattered is beyond me, but the point is, I met him about three months into his 32nd year of life. Although he was much older than the people I usually hung out with and even though he dressed kind of like an old man, he was charming and he wooed me. Nine months later, on the night of his 33rd birthday, he proposed and I said yes. I'm sure there were romantic gestures and fun moments, but the gist of it is I ended up with a ring on my finger and my feet in the stirrups twenty-two months after I said, "I do."

He has never been a hands-on dad and between his pursuits as a small business owner and his love of the game of golf, he is not around much. When he is, it usually means he will take the kids "off my hands" for a few hours, only to return within ninety minutes claiming some "emergency" at one of the businesses. His disheveled appearance (ketchup down the front of his favorite golfing vest) and panicked look speak volumes to the "emergency," but it has never bothered me much that he isn't around because I am having too much fun raising good little people and enjoying spending my time with them. My life is filled and made complete by my kids.

We lead very separate lives and although we rarely (if ever) fight, we also rarely speak to one another. Beyond exchanges pertaining to the kids, schedules and money, there is not much resembling a marriage within the walls of our house. I'm OK with playing the role of "wife," throwing parties like our Thanksgiving celebration in the hope of strengthening the bonds between family and friends. My marriage may not provide me with much support or friendship, but I have filled my life (and the lives of my children) with people that offer plenty of both.

Hopefully as I move forward in sharing my journey, you will now have a better understanding of who I am, where I come from, and how I got to where I am now.

Chapter Three

I Can't Fight This Feeling Anymore

"The best thing is to not think about what other people can do, but instead think about what you are going to accomplish next."

Six months ago, I was sitting on the beach in Martha's Vineyard. I was at the water's edge watching the kids jump and play in the waves. As the bubbly water gently crashed around my toes and feet, I knew that it should feel cold, that I should notice when the water rolled over them. But there was nothing but a heavy dead feeling. My right foot was far worse than the left. The left seemed to occasionally remember that it was supposed to be feeling cold. But my right foot was completely numb and felt "dead."

The only way I can try and explain it is that heavy/dead/numb feeling you get if your foot falls asleep. Maybe you had it curled up all cock-eyed underneath you and when you try and release it, there might be one or two pins or a few needles. But, if you are very careful, to not shake or bump your foot, to not disturb its slumber, there is a feeling. A dead or numb feeling, as if that part of your body is no longer working in conjunction with the rest of your body and your brain. Then you shake your foot, or stomp it on the ground, tensing in anticipation for the shooting pokes and stabs that come with waking your slumbering body part.

That's what it felt like. But I never got the pins and needles. My foot seemed to stay in hibernation that day, and for many more days this past summer. Given that I had gone for my daily run (a loop out around West Chop, back down Franklin Ave. to the center of town and then back to my folks' home in the woods), I hardly thought it was something horrid or drastic. More than likely, just a pinched nerve. Certainly annoying, but nothing to worry about… or so I thought.

There have been other things. Other symptoms that I can't explain. I sometimes have these crazy electric shock feelings run up my spine when I am in the shower (again, could be a nerve?). A few times this summer, I recall my vision seeming to get blurry. But then again, that could so easily have been me smudging my contact lens with sunscreen or getting salt water on them. So, still nothing to be overly concerned or alarmed about.

I didn't mention any of this to anyone, choosing to follow one of my favorite life quotes, "ignore it and it will go away." But by the end of the summer, I ended up back here in Seattle and the symptoms grew worse and started to affect my left foot as well. It seemed to be spreading and it seemed to be more severe and higher up on my right side. I still didn't tell any of my family and friends or my husband, because I wanted to believe it was just that stupid pinched nerve. Because it could totally be a nerve. That's what I kept telling myself, but concern began to creep in, so I made an appointment with a doctor.

I have always been healthy. I don't have a "regular" doctor per se, but I do have a close relationship with my OB-GYN, thanks to the birth of my three children. So the doctor I went to see (a general internist) didn't know much of anything about me when I arrived for the appointment. Based on how young and healthy I looked, she didn't seem overly concerned when I described my symptoms, but she did say she wanted to set up an appointment for me to have an EEG in the neurology department.

This was the moment a little alarm began to go off in my mind. EEG?!?! Neurology department?!?! These are serious medical terms!!!! Is this something serious!?!?! Am I dying?!?!

My mind raced as I waited for the doctor to come back in. I remember thinking, "is this something that I am going to have to tell people about? Is this something that is going to change my life?"

I learned that neurology is a very popular and busy business. The department at the hospital was so backed up that my appointment was scheduled for three weeks out. Given the business of the department and the fact that it pertains to really serious and important medical stuff, I took this as a good sign. If the doctor felt it was okay to wait three weeks, then I certainly must not be dying, at least not in the immediate future.

Two days prior to the appointment, I had a message on my answering machine. It was the hospital. It was about my appointment for the EEG. Apparently the doctor who was supposed perform the test broke his arm and my appointment had been cancelled. Rather than leaving a call back number, the voice on my machine assured me that someone would call to reschedule. I waited, a day, then two, then a week. Unsure what the appropriate protocol for calling an unresponsive neurological department back is, I decided to just ignore it all, again. I figured if they weren't worried, why should I?

Ignore all I want, the symptoms continued and were getting more severe. I'm a stubborn and willful person, and if I say I am going to ignore something, than goddamn it, I am ignoring it! And I did, until I peed my pants on the playground while waiting for my kids to be let out of school. Fortunately for me, it was a beautiful Indian summer day and I was still outfitted in my summer attire, a sun dress and flip-flops.

It was a surreal experience. There was no indication that I had to pee, no fleeting thought of, "oh crap, I've got to go to the bathroom." No warning! No prior knowledge whatsoever of what was to come. One minute, I was standing there talking to a few of the other pick-up parents and the next I looked down to discover, "Holy crap, I'm peeing!" Thankfully my summer clothing allowed me to

23

avoid the absolute shame and embarrassment of having just wet my-self in front of other fully functioning members of society, parents of my children's friends, people I know! The pee just quietly fell to the wood chips that cover the playground and no one even noticed as I entered into full and complete panic mode.

That night, I made an unexpected call. To my husband, at work. I had been consumed with thoughts about what could be wrong with me since I arrived home from picking the kids up. After bath and book time, I had tucked the kids into their beds and gone to curl up in the chair that is in the corner of our master bedroom. It is where I used to curl up with my children, when they were little babies. If they were fussy and I couldn't get them to settle back to sleep after a feeding, I would move over to this big comfy chair, eventually nodding off for the night with a baby in my arms.

Despite the warm day, the night had brought in the expected Sep-tember chill, so I grabbed a blanket as I dialed the number. Through tears and sobs, I told him what had been going on. I told him about the dead feet, electric shocks, blurry vision and peeing. Having not said anything at all up until that moment, he was more than a bit surprised and confused by my call and the information I spewed at him. He assured me that everything was going to be alright. I'm not sure I believed him. But at least I had told someone. That made it seem more real. That made it seem like it was something I could no longer ignore.

One of the new symptoms that I had been experiencing is a tightening around my midsection. An odd, and not very pleasant squeeze. The only thing I could equate it to is the feeling of the baby moving in my belly when I was pregnant, so I decided to go and see my OB-GYN. After having three babies, we are close. Over the course of a sleepless night, I convinced myself that I had a massive tumor in my uterus that was pushing up against my spinal cord and causing the symptoms. It was the tumor's fault I had peed myself in public!

My regular OB-GYN was not available, but I was able to convey my urgency in seeing someone as soon as possible. It may have been the sobs and hysteria I lamely tried to conceal but for whatever reason, the nurse on the phone the next morning seemed to sense my level of alarm and she found an appointment with another doctor in the office for the very next day.

I am well aware that beggars can't be choosers (another favorite life quote of mine) but I did have a moment's hesitation when the doctor walked into the exam room. She was young. Like really young. I realize that I am no spring chicken these days and that my judgement of age seems to get more distorted with every passing year, but I was pretty sure that there is no way the young woman that stood in front of me could not have had time to complete medical school, and all the other crap they have to do before becoming real doctors, Not at her age.

But who was I to judge? I had a medical crisis going on, and if she was willing to listen, I was willing to spill. And spill I did. Within mere moments of her arrival, I was bawling my eyes out, describing my symptoms and telling her that I knew that I have a tumor or something else just as severely wrong with my uterus.

She was wonderful and understanding, but she quickly explained that when not pregnant, my uterus is about the size of my fist and sits low down on my pelvic bone. It might be time to mention that I am not a medical professional, so this may not be completely accurate, or accurate at all, but it is what I remember from the appointment. She assured me that the tightening sensation I was feeling was not in fact the tumor I had self diagnosed, but something completely different. She explained that based on what I had been describing, it was clearly a neurological episode, and she assured me that she would get me to the right person, and fast! At that moment, I realized I didn't care if I was dealing with the female version of Doogie Howser—she believed me and she was going to get me help!

I left her office with the names and numbers of two neurologists scribbled on an appointment card that I fidgeted with as I walked somewhat aimlessly into the parking garage towards my car. I climbed into the driver's seat, flopped open my bag and reached for my wallet. I needed to call my insurance company to find out if either of the doctors listed on the now frayed card were on our preferred provider list, and whether I would need to have a referral or prior authorization in order for the expenses to be covered.

This shit was getting real! Thoughts of a pinched nerve and it not being a big deal were long gone and I found myself constantly fighting off a huge wave of sheer and utter panic. I kept thinking, "What the fuck is wrong with me?!?!?"

Apparently neurology was still a busy industry. Similar to back in early fall when the first doctor I saw tried to get me an appointment, I was told the first available appointment would be two weeks out. If you have ever had some medical issue happen to you, if you have had something wrong and not known what it is then you know the all-consuming urgency you feel to see someone now! So while still in my car, returning from my OB-GYN's office, I decided to try and reach the doctor that I had seen back in September.

The stars must have been in alignment for me that day, because not only was she in, but was available to see me in an hour! (Good thing I was still in the car.) I was finally ready to admit that there was something more than a pinched nerve wrong with me and I hoped that I had found people that believed me and would help me.

She remembered me, and the minute she walked in, she had asked about the neurologist, the EEG and what I had learned. I explained about the broken arm, cancelled appointment, no call back thing and again I broke down in tears. She sat in the molded chair accompanying mine next to a built-in desk where there are various pamphlets and a jar with q-tips. She reached out and took my hand. As she held it and gave it a squeeze, she assured me that she would get me in to see

26

someone there at the hospital, that day—within hours! I found myself flooded with relief and a sense of calm. She had listened to me. She had believed me and she was going to get me help!

Apparently kindness and caring don't always carry enough weight to get one in to see a neurologist in this particular hospital. She was told that the first available appointment was in four days. I heard her sternly and clearly state that this was not unacceptable, and thought, "see, she is worried! It IS something!" She was told it was the best that could be done and she abruptly hung up. She mumbled a few words of frustration, then looked at me, directly in my eyes, and again promised that she was going to help me. She left the office for a few minutes and returned with a post-it note. Another doctor's name and another number. She explained that he had been recommended to her by one of her friends from medical school. She said that she had already called the office and they would see me the next day. I was in!

Chapter Four

Losing My MRI Virginity

"Remember 40-year-old virgin?
You can be the "hot" grandma."

As I have mentioned, I am a fairly physically fit thirty-seven-year old woman. I am blessed with average good looks, an "interesting but pleasant" style of dress, a natural tendency to smile and a strong desire to put people at ease. I am sharing this now because it may help you get a sense of what people's first impression of me might be, and what the doctor was met with the following day.

The office was located in a small building on the grounds of the hospital, and when I walk in, it reminded me of my orthodontist's office (flashbacks to being fourteen.) It's not unpleasant, just extremely outdated. There were no computers or monitors in sight. A large appointment book lay on the surface just below the check-in window. As I quietly gave the young gal with purple hair and a nose ring my name, I saw her make a neat little check mark in the empty box besides my appointment time. Check. I had made it. I had arrived.

When the doctor entered the room, I estimated that he was about my age. He was an attractive guy and I immediately sensed that he might suffer from a bit of a doctor complex, but nothing too extreme or off-putting. (Talk about first impressions, and I was worried about him judging me.) I was seated in a chair beside his bigger-than-the-room-needs sized desk. It seemed to be in a battle for space with various boxes and stacks of files and books and I'm not sure which was winning.

He asked about my symptoms and I began to try to put into words all the things that I have been feeling, all the things that have happened since that first day, back when I was on the beach and simply waiting for the cold water to hit my feet. He interrupted my retelling of the story that has been my life over the past few months with seemingly irrelevant and insignificant questions and then promptly asked me to step next door, into an exam room and to put on one of those beloved ass-revealing gowns.

I have never had a neurological exam. I didn't know what to expect, but given that "neurological" is a big, impressive word, I was anticipating big, impressive things. The exam consisted of the doctor banging on my knees with a hammer type thing, using a tuning fork on my toes, asking me to push against his hands with my feet, and instructing me to walk in a straight line down the office hallway. It did cross my mind as I wobbled down hallway, head down, eyes focused on the dingy office tweed carpet, "Why would they insist on me wearing the ass-revealing gown and then ask for such an ego-destroying feat? I already stumble like a damn drunk, now my ass needs to be flapping in the wind while I try and just make it to the end of the damn hallway?"

The exam ended with the doctor asking me to close my eyes and touch my nose. That was it. No big machines or complicated tests.

He didn't say much of anything about whether I was passing the tests, but I didn't know him, maybe he is just the silent type? He nodded encouragement as I performed each task. He then told me to get dressed and meet him back in his office. As the door shut behind him, I was left in the exam room, with my ass out and my mouth wide open. What just happened? How could what we had done lead him to know anything about me, my life, or the hell I have been going through? As I pulled the zipper up on my boot, I thought to myself, "this guy has no fucking clue!"

I arranged myself to look calm, cool and collected on the same chair next to the too-big-for-the-room desk. There was a knock at the door, immediately followed by his entry into the office. He stepped gingerly around the boxes and piles and settled himself back behind the desk. Steepling his hands in front of his face, he looked at me and announced that he has good news and bad news.

Oh shit! Did I want to hear this? Did I really want to know what has been wrong for all these months if it's bad? I wanted to ask which one is the more important piece of news? Which one is going to matter more: the good or the bad news? Why the fuck didn't I bring some-one with me to this appointment? What if it is earth-shattering? Life changing? I'm going to be sitting here, with a complete stranger and I might lose it! I might not be able to handle this. What had I been thinking? I took a deep breath and asked him to elaborate.

He told me I have Transverse Myelitis. The good news was it is a temporary condition. It is contracted from a virus; something any of my kids could have picked up and shared with me. He explained that it had caused spots of unwanted fluid in my spinal cord.

"If you think of your spinal cord like an electrical cord," he told me, "water (the fluid) will cause shorts in the wiring." According to his diagnosis, this was what was causing the symptoms that I had been experiencing.

He told me that it will go away.

The bad news was that it could take up to a year for it to get better. I must admit, I was more than a bit skeptical that he had ascertained all of this from the tuning fork, hammer, sobriety test episode in the other room. He, then, explained that he wanted me to get a thoracic MRI, so that he could see exactly where the fluid is and how much is in there.

This is a lot of shit going down!

First a neurologist, and now an MRI? Whatever the hell that is! I don't know about these things! I have always been healthy. The only time I visit doctors is when I am making babies!

He seemed to make the assumption that I had even a clue about what he had been rambling on about and I simply nodded in agreement. He was a doctor, he knows what he is doing, and he is going to help me and make all this crap go away. I am going to be able to be me again. I am not going to have to stomp my foot or pee my pants in public forever because he is going to take care of me. Make me better. That is what I hear him saying to me.

We set up an appointment with the hospital for the following day and I headed back to the parking lot, completely unaware of the rain that had begun to fall. As I merged onto I-5, my mind went over what had transpired in the past hour. I had met a doctor that had a rubber hammer and tuning fork. I had walked down a hallway, flashing my ass for the world to see. I touched my finger to my nose, over and over again. All of that had led the doctor to believe that I have this weird named thing/condition/disease?

I wasn't even sure what "it" is. I began to berate myself for not asking more questions. I then realized that there is a good chance that I wouldn't even remember the name of it by the time I made it home. As I headed for the ramp onto 520, I punched the gas, hoping to make it there before I forgot what the doctor told me.

Given my sobbing confession a few nights earlier, my husband obviously knew that I had been to the neurologist, but I didn't tell anyone else. No other family or friends. I am close to my parents, and I did wonder why I hadn't told them. Prior to my sobbing phone call, I hadn't told anyone; once I had seen the OB-GYN and she had said I needed to see a neurologist, I felt I wanted to wait and find out what was wrong before telling anyone. I hated the idea of anyone worrying about me. I also rationalized that it would be much easier to explain it if I knew what "it" was, if I already knew what was wrong with me and why I have been having weird things happen.

That night, as I curled up on the big chair to call my parents, I felt a tinge of guilt, for keeping them in the dark for so long. I tried to start from the beginning, to explain all the things that I had been feeling and the things that had been happening with my body. It was a lot for them to take in. I knew that they were mad and sad that I hadn't told them, that I had kept it all to myself and had been going through this alone. They were extremely concerned, but given what the doctor told me, I assured them that all was well, and I promised I would call again once I had the MRI results.

It was 8:10 a.m. when I dropped the kids off at school and 8:15 as I wound my way through the Arboretum, headed to I-5 to find my way back to the hospital. It had been a long and sleepless night, lying in bed thinking about what the doctor said and worrying about the MRI. To be honest, I still didn't really know what an MRI was, or what it would entail. I had certainly heard the term before and I vaguely recall it involving a bed that goes into a tube. But that was about it.

I knew I could have done a search on the internet but I didn't. Truthfully, I didn't trust jumping on the internet. I feared that I would enter the "black vortex" of medical terms and conditions and self diagnose with something far worse than the originally feared uterus tumor. Or worse yet: completely freak myself out over the procedure that I was committed to having in the morning. Instead, I spent the night tossing and turning and just wanting it to be over. I just wanted to be "normal" again.

As I pulled Bessy into the parking lot, it was pouring rain. The cold, wet, gray day seemed to mirror my mood. The thought of being strapped down and put in a tube was daunting to say the least and I was more than just a bit apprehensive about what I was getting myself into. As I climbed out of the car and adjusted my skirt, I pulled my coat tight around my body and put on my "I must feel good, because I look good" smile and headed into the waiting room.

Once I had given my name and date of birth to the receptionist, I was handed a clipboard with a bunch of forms to fill out. As I settled into one of the many empty chairs, I took ahold of the flower adorned pen that was chained to the clipboard and began to fill in the blanks. The questions started out basic enough; name, age, date of birth, address. I was nailing it! I wasn't even phased by #8) Allergies to medications? I had neatly printed "NONE," in all caps, to clearly depict that really there isn't anything wrong with me.

Then came the more difficult questions. The ones I was not prepared for, the ones that I didn't know the answers to. Well, technically I did know the answers, but I was quickly second guessing myself as I read on the form that an MRI is a giant magnet.

Do you have any metal implanted in your body?

To the best of my knowledge, I don't, but when faced with a giant magnet, my mind began to race. Maybe I did have metal in my body and I just don't remember! I had tubes put in my ears when I was four, and for years I have been told that they fell out about six months after the procedure (which is normal). But what if they didn't fall out? I am pretty sure they were plastic, but what if I am wrong? What if they hadn't fallen out and have remained there, silently, for all these years, undetected because no one has been probing and searching in my ears? (My vagina, having had three kids, yes; ears, no.) What if they were metal and not plastic and then I am put in this giant magnetic tube and they are sucked out of my head?

I know this all sounds crazy, but these were the things that were running through my mind while sitting in that waiting room.

The other question that appeared on the form a few times was, "are you claustrophobic?"

I honestly don't know the answer to that question, because I have always had a fear that I might be, so I have avoided being in any situation that might lead to me discovering that I am. Really, how do I answer that question if I have never had a chance to test the theory? It took me far too long to complete the forms as I checked and unchecked the "Y" next to the Claustrophobia question at least ten times. I didn't know what the "right" answer was! This seemed like a fairly important question given the impending tube and I didn't know the answer!

I finally decided that the answer was, "No"—I am not claustrophobic—simply because I didn't want to be. I didn't have the time or energy to be worrying about this "might-be" scenario. There was something wrong with me and I needed to just suck it up and get on with the MRI so that I could get better.

I handed my completed forms back to the receptionist and shortly after a young man popped out of a door to the left of where she was sitting and whispered, "Megan? Megan Lewellyn?" "Oh shit... it was time", I think, as I was led back to a changing room. He instructed me to take everything but my underwear off and explained locking my belongings up in one of the lockers located on the wall just to my left.

As I tucked my earrings, bracelets, necklaces and rings into the toe of my boot, I ran my hands over my almost naked body in search of any forgotten jewelry, my mind returned to the question about metal and my long ago ear tubes. It all sounds crazy and ludicrous and I knew I was not thinking clearly or logically, but here is the thing; nothing about this was "logical," none of it made any sense. I am not a sick person. Things like this, major medical procedures don't happen to me. So I can't really blame my mind for deciding to take off on some journey about a long forgotten tube.

A light knock on the door indicated that they were waiting for me. They were ready to get on with the procedure, but I wasn't sure I was ready. On so many different levels, I just wanted it all to stop. I wanted the stomping dead-foot, uncontrolled peeing and weird and uncomfortable sensations in my legs to stop. I didn't want to be at the hospital. I didn't want to be in yet another ass-baring gown, and I sure as hell didn't want to be strapped to something and sent into a giant tube. I didn't want any of this! I stood, greeted the nurse at the door and slowly followed him into the MRI room, where I encountered my first MRI machine.

It was a tube—a big one, with a bed on sliders to move in and out of the concave world inside of the tube. As I sat on the edge of the bed a technician entered the room and as the nurse handed him my forms, he smiled and approached me.

Making eye contact, he introduced himself, "Hi, I'm Brian, and I'll be performing your MRI today." Toward the end of the sentence, his eyes had drifted to my file that now sat in his hands. Looking over the forms he released a loud "hhhhhmmmmm." Let me assure you that this is not a sound you want to hear anyone make when you are about to undertake the most significant medical procedure of your life.

Brian then asked, "Just a thoracic? Don't you want to get a head scan as well?"

What the fuck? Literally WTF!?!?!

How the hell would I know?!?! "Come to think of it, Brian, I actually don't WANT to be getting any part of my body scanned! I don't want to be here! I don't want to be sick and I sure as hell don't want my body to be fucked up anymore. So I don't know, Brian! I don't know if I *want* a brain scan—I am here because my doctor told me to be here, but that is really all I know."

I think Brian sensed I was a bit stressed.

I made a deal with my body as the bed slid into the cavity of the machine. If I kept my eyes shut (completely shut) the whole time, then I wouldn't see that I was confined to such a small and uncomfortable space. That is how I was going to avoid freaking out.

The whole procedure took about fifty-five minutes. It was loud as hell, and telling me to not move, not even to itch my nose, had been a guarantee that my nose itched like crazy the entire time (Thanks a lot Brian!). Apparently I am not claustrophobic, but it took all of my will power to breathe through the panic that lay just below the surface of my rational thinking. I spent a lot of time thinking about not panicking, about not freaking out, which in some ways was a nice break from constantly thinking about what could be wrong with me. While in the machine, I had no mental space to worry about why I was there; I only focused on not moving, making it through the procedure, and not completely losing it!

There was only one break in the relentless whirring, beeps and grunts the machine made. I heard the Brian's voice pumped into the tube. He explained that he would be sliding me out to administer what he called an enhancing agent. He also mentioned it was contrast. I remember thinking, "I really should have spent some time on the internet reading about MRIs, but obviously it was a little bit late for that."

"Out?" Out sounded good to me, even if it meant that he would be poking me with another needle.

Enhancing agent in, needle out and I was immediately slid back into the gaping mouth of the machine. As I squeezed my eyes shut for the second time my head entered the muted world of the tube, I could feel the panic begin to swell. I wasn't sure how much more of it I could take. When I heard the voice again, it assured me that I was, "just about" done. I didn't believe him. Because "just about" is not calculable. It does not tell me how many more times I need to count backwards from one hundred, or try and say the alphabet in reverse. "Just about" is worse than "almost" because "almost" gives an unspoken nod to an end. "Just about" makes it sound as if really no one knows how long it will be and so let's just use vague terms that make no promises.

Eventually it was over and I am pretty sure that I snarled at Brian when he came to retrieve me. I know that it's not his fault, that none of this has anything to do with him, but he was an available target and I was maxed out as far as trying to stay in control and not lose it.

I had an appointment with Dr. K. a bit later that day and although I felt more than a bit overwhelmed and exhausted from the mental process of making it through the MRI procedure, I decided that what I needed was normalcy, for my life to stop looking like something out of a medical TV show and just be back to the way it has always been. What better way to do that than to use the time to check a few things off my to-do list (laundry detergent, dog food, toothpaste, etc.). I found myself, yet again, maneuvering Bessy through the parking lot at Target.

About an hour into my shopping, my cell phone rang. It was Dr. K.—it was actually him, and not a nurse or secretary. This had set off the alarms again!

He explained that he was looking at the results and that he wanted me to go back to the lab and have a brain scan done. I guess I should have listened to Brian! My heart began to race! What did he see that has led him to wanting me to go back in that God awful contraption?

When I posed this question to him (not quite in so many words), he explained that although what he was seeing was what he expected, he wanted to get a look at the brain as well "just to see."

"Just to see?!" That sounded no better than "just about." I was quickly beginning to dislike the word "just."

My gut reaction was to say "tough luck, asshole! You should have thought of this before you sent me into the tube." I politely declined. When I said, "no thanks", Dr. K. seemed to be a bit baffled. (I'm not sure he is used to being told "no"). I explained that I had done what he asked of me, this big enormous thing, and I survived. I told him that I was now at Target getting things on my list as if this should be reason enough to not go back into the tube.

He informed me that I needed to check out and head back immediately to have a second scan. Did this man have any idea how valuable a few kid-free hours can be to a mother with a huge to-do list? I begrudgingly followed his orders and headed to the checkout line. Just as I was paying for the purchases (about half of what I needed to get), my phone rang. It was Dr. K. again. This time he told me that he had tried to book me back into the MRI lab, but learned that they can't perform the brain scan due to the enhancer that they had administered. (I had to wait twenty-four hours for it to clear out of my system.) I had let out a small laugh when I thought, "Yes! Saved by the needle!"

We agreed that I would still come back to his office for my appointment in about an hour.

Back in his office, he had been reviewing the scan on his computer and he tried to direct the screen towards me so I could look. He pointed out the areas with fluid and explained that although this is the results he expected to see, he wanted to get a look at my brain as well.

I would like to think that I am not a difficult patient, but I also am not one to jump at any medical procedure without a good reason. My thoughts at this point were, why go through another scan if what he is looking at is what he expected? Why not wait and see if my symptoms begin to improve (as he said they would) rather than spending more money for what seemed to me to be just a "looksy." He must have been anticipating my response (perhaps due to our phone conversation when I was in Target) because he immediately countered with, "okay, I'll trade you a brain scan for a spinal tap."

A number of thoughts ran through my head at this proposal. First, is this poker? Second, what do I really know about this doctor? Third, maybe I should get a second opinion?

Similar to my response to the proposed brain scan, I responded with a "thanks, but no." When he asked why I wouldn't agree to the spinal tap, I had simply explained, "because they hurt!" He assured me that they don't, but when I inquired as to whether he has ever had one, he responded, "no." Hah! At least I've had an epidural, not the same, but close in my mind, and that hurt a lot!

I explained to Dr. K. that although I am not trying to be difficult, I didn't want to just go willy nilly with the tests with no good reason behind them. My logic was, since what he saw was indicative of Transverse Myelitis, and it is something that will heal over time, why not wait and see if that is the case? He begrudgingly agreed.

As I left the office, I remember thinking, "a year's not so long, especially if I begin to improve over time and return to my "normal" self at the end."

Within weeks, my symptoms took a turn for the worse and I was really struggling to walk and keep my balance. I had a few falls around the house. Nothing earth shattering, but they shook me up. So about two weeks after walking out of Dr. Krane's office, turning down his poker deal, I called back. With my tail between my legs, I explained to the nurse that I was getting worse and that I wanted to make a deal.

I agreed to the spinal tap.

Chapter Five

Spinal Tap with an "American Idiot"

"From what I can deduce (police skill) you have some very good friends. Friends are important because they tell you like it is. And they provide the shoulder needed to lean on."

Deciding on what underwear to wear for my first ever spinal tap proved to be a bit challenging. A thong was certainly out of the question, but so too were my ever loved Spanks and other granny-like panties that I may or may not have stuffed in my "unmentionables" drawer. What does one wear to have a large needle shoved into one's back? Standard cotton briefs? Too boring. But certainly not anything lacy or sexy—that would just be awkward. I finally decided on a pair of boy briefs, adequate coverage with a nod to sporty. I won't tell you just how long I spent on this dilemma. Others might worry about having an incurable disease, but me: I worry about a doctor looking at my ass as I curl up in a fetal position on a hospital bed and wanting it to look as good as possible.

Dr. K. (whom I now think of as my "Poker Playing" doctor) had offered to do the procedure during his lunch hour. I didn't know if this was a lame attempt at making up for trying to play poker with my medical treatments? Maybe I had managed to convince him that juggling my schedule around three kids and all their activities is challenging to say the least? Maybe he just wanted to see my ass? Whatever the reason for this "generous" offer, it meant that I was once again in Bessy, heading north on I-5 after dropping the kids off at school.

After I checked in, I changed into yet another backless hospital gown and climbed into bed. I didn't have to wait long for there to be a gentle knock at the door. The "Poker Playing" doctor arrived with a rolling cart, upon which sat a number of small vials and a big ass needle.

Holy shit!! Breathe!!

Once again, all of this was getting really real!

Why the fuck didn't I at least look up the doctor on the internet? Why hadn't I taken the time to find out if he is considered a "good" doctor? Did he even know what he was doing? Had he really ever done this procedure before? It is a really big needle and I was definitely having second thoughts.

I can't really speak to his bedside manner—because there wasn't any. No small talk (or foreplay, if you will). He explained that it was imperative that I stay absolutely still and he said that the procedure should take about ten minutes once he put the needle in and had begun to extract my spinal fluid.

The first hint that the "Poker Playing" doctor might be a liar was when the needle went in. I recall very clearly that he said that it wouldn't hurt. Why the fuck had I believed him??? Logic would dictate that ramming a long sharp needle into my spine would definitely hurt... and it did! I'm not going to lie. Knowing that if I moved, I might cause severe and permanent damage (his words, not mine) magnified the discomfort and sheer terror that I felt. I remember thinking, "why the fuck did I choose to do this on my own?!" Squeezing the shit out of someone's hand had done amazing things to help with the pain of labor, I needed someone's hand to squeeze. But as always, I was alone and left to my own devices to get through yet another procedure.

Fortunately, I had brought my iPod and I turned it on just before the doctor started the procedure. I didn't pay attention to what I would be listening to, I just knew I wanted it loud! Something to distract me from where I was and what I was going through. As the first song ended and then began again, I realized my error. It was on repeat and given my current situation, rolling over to rectify the situation was out of the question. So I listened to "American Idiot" by Green Day the entire time.

As the "Poker Playing" doctor pulled the needle out, he snapped off his latex gloves and announced that we were all done. He then asked what I had been listening to. When I told him the title of the song, he smiled slightly and said, "ah, a song about your doctor; good choice."

The needle was out, my spinal fluid had been packed up and was ready to be sent off to the Mayo Clinic for analysis. He explained that he would be testing for a number of different conditions in the hope of ruling out all of the possibilities. Given that we were at the start of Thanksgiving week, he estimated that he wouldn't get the results back until the following week. He spent a bit of time explaining about a possible side effects of the tap, something about the hole in my spine where the needle had intruded not healing up, leaking fluid and a headache. I was vaguely aware of what he was saying, but I took solace in the fact that all the information and instructions he was imparting upon me are neatly outlined on the sheet of paper he handed me, just before exiting the room.

I quickly got dressed, hit Target once again and then headed for the highway to pick up the kids. Other than a slight tenderness in my lower back, I felt fine as I pulled into the dreaded pick-up line to await the final bell and the inevitable explosion of noise and little bodies to erupt from the building.

I continued to feel great throughout the weekend—that is until Sunday night. It was 7:30 p.m., my husband was nowhere to be found and I had to get the kids fed and into bed since it was a school night, but my head was throbbing. It had started a few hours earlier, just a slight tinge of pain that I chocked up to being out and about with the kids all day, and not eating enough. But over the next few hours, it had gotten progressively worse, and I was now at the point where the task of simply boiling water for mac 'n cheese seemed absolutely daunting —if not impossible.

I began frantically searching for the nice informative piece of paper "Poker Playing" doctor had handed me and after about 15 minutes of tearing apart every square inch of the kitchen (I knew it was there somewhere), I finally located it under a pile of rocks and grass that Max had dragged in from the yard. (Don't ask—he's a nature boy these days—I was just lucky there weren't any ants, caterpillars or slugs in the pile).

I quickly scanned the sheet and read about this now not-so-elusive headache the doctor had mentioned. The information stated, "some patients experience a sharp headache minutes or hours after having the procedure." There was no mention of four days later. In the instructions, it said that lying down could significantly help with alleviating the pain. So I stumbled over the couch and laid down.

You need to know that this is not something that I normally do, I don't just plop down on the couch for a rest, and certainly not right smack in the middle of dinner preparations, so my arrival on the couch, where the kids were curled up watching TV was sure to raise an alarm for them. They knew that there had been something going on. I had explained to them that, "mommy's body isn't working the way it is supposed to" and I had told them that I had been to see a doctor about it all. But now, there I was, lying prone on the couch, next to their warm little bodies, as the water for the mac 'n cheese came to a violent boil on the stove top.

I'll be damned if they aren't right—shortly after I lay down, the pounding began to recede. Within twenty minutes, I felt ok again. So I popped up, to finish making dinner. Which was a bad idea. It only took about ten minutes for the pain to return and it seemed to be even worse the second time. I turned the water off, grabbed the sheet of paper and the cordless phone, and headed back to the couch.

Thirty minutes later, I was on the phone with an "on-call" doctor, having followed the instructions on the sheet and called the hospital where the "Poker Playing" doctor works. I had explained to him that I had a spinal tap and now was experiencing an excruciating head-ache. He explained that in a normal situation, the hole that the needle made in my spinal cord would seal up on its own. He used a cut on your finger as an example. The blood begins to dry up and forms a scab. This is what my spinal cord was supposed to do, but apparently not. It seems my spinal cord is just one more part of my body that had decided to let me down.

When I tell him that I had the tap four days ago—he tells me that's not possible.

Huh? Excuse me? And why would I lie about this?

The conversation spiraled from there. He insisted that I come into the ER immediately to have a spinal patch (yet another thing I know nothing about). I explained that wasn't possible and I began to list off all the shit I had to get done. I mentioned I had three kids, and no one to watch them if I were to leave.

I sensed that the doctor on-call was not used to having patients refuse his orders and certainly not ones that have called into the hospital's after-hours emergency line, which is how I ended up on the phone with him in the first place. I was on the phone, arguing about not going to the hospital that I, myself, had called.

"Let me ask you this. Is this lack of fluid causing any damage to my brain as it hits up against my skull?" (This was my translation of what I had read on the information sheet as I lay on the couch waiting for the doctor on-call to call me).

47

"Permanent? No."

"Is it causing temporary damage?"

"No, no damage to speak of, but…"

I cut in there, seeing my opening and going for it.

"So, if I were able to make it through the night, because I will be lying down for a better part of it, and came into the hospital during normal business hours (aka after I drop the kids off at school) and requested a spinal patch, it would be no different than me coming in right now to have the procedure?"

"Different, no; it would be the same. But I don't think that you are taking into account the pain…"

Again, I had to interrupt, because who the fuck is he to say that I am not taking into account the pain?! I am the one in pain—what the hell does he know about my pain!?

I took a deep breath and politely assured the doctor on-call that I was certain I could make it through the night. I promised him that I would head to the hospital first thing in the morning, and I hung up.

I stood up and quickly put my plan into action—because of course I had a plan. I always have a plan, that is how I get everything done. While I was on the phone with the doctor on-call I had stood up, to try and see about dinner. The relief that I experienced when lying down had lingered a bit. It wasn't as if I stood up and bam the pain was back. It definitely began to worsen the moment I stood up, but it had been bearable for about ten minutes—just enough time for me to cook the pasta and dump it in the colander before stumbling back to my spot on the couch.

So, while I argued with the doctor on the phone, I had been mapping out my evening in chunks of ten minute activities and I was now eager to get on with it—with the thought of the blissful relief I would experience once I could sink down into my own bed and not stand up every ten minutes driving me forward.

I spent the first ten minutes of standing finishing up the mac 'n cheese and throwing some veggies on plates and getting the kids sitting down and eating dinner. Then I laid down. I spent my next ten minutes cleaning up the dishes and getting the kids upstairs, where I promptly laid down again. I'm pretty sure my kids hadn't seen me lying down this many times in their entire lives. I put them to bed each night and I am there to greet them when they wake in the morning. Lying down is not something I do.

I spent the next allotment of "standing time" filling the bathtub and getting all three kids through the fastest bath of their lives, into their pjs and into my bedroom, where I lay down... and curled up with all three of them and I read them a few books. I, then, got each of the kids snuggled into their own beds, popped my contacts out, brushed my teeth and climbed into bed, head pounding and exhausted. Apparently, it takes a lot of energy to fight off pain. As I rolled over to try and find a position that caused the least amount of discomfort to my throbbing head, I remember thinking, "I have no idea where my husband is."

I woke in the morning and rolled over to find the other side of the bed still empty. As I lay there, thinking about getting up and what lay ahead in the day, I thought about how nice it would be to have someone on my team. Someone who could help me get through all of this shit. Someone who I could talk to about how scary this has all been. I was tired of trying to deal with it on my own. I was tired of being alone.

As I thought through my plan for the day, I realized the part that was a bit risky was that I was assuming that after a good night's sleep, and lying down for 8+ hours, that the relief would last longer than when I was lying down for ten minutes to stand up for ten minutes. But I didn't know that for a fact. I set my alarm for the latest possible time, to still get the kids up and out for school, but to maximize my time being horizontal.

The alarm had gone off at 7:30, and I slowly sat up and turned to put my feet on the floor. The pain had been almost non-existent—a good first step to what I knew is going to be a long morning. I woke the kids and head downstairs to feed the dogs and let them out in the back-yard. I had to assume that the kids were worried about me, because they all arrive in the kitchen, dressed and carrying their backpacks just minutes after I got downstairs. Although I was incredibly grateful for this small miracle, I couldn't help but think, "Really?! Really?! Every morning it takes every ounce of my energy and creative parenting to get these three up, dressed, fed and out the door, with constant reminders and redirections barked out by yours truly. And now here they were, all ready to go, and I didn't have to do jack-shit?!"

We headed out to the garage and the kids climbed into their seats in the back of the van, plopping their packs and lunch bins on the floor beside the sliding door. I hit the garage door opener, put Bessy into reverse, and quickly glanced at the clock on the dashboard, before turning to look as I backed out of the garage. It was 8:15—I had been vertical for just over forty-five minutes. The pain had returned, actually it returned about twenty minutes after I climbed out of bed and it had been a gradual escalation, but it was getting bad.

Ten minutes later, as I heard the loud thunk of the sliding door being shut by Sam and I waved goodbye to the kids as they ran up the hill and into the school yard, I thought, there is no way that I am going to make it to the hospital. It's a thirty-five minute drive, without traffic, and there wasn't a chance in hell that there wasn't traffic on I-5 North at 8:30 on a Monday morning. I thought about returning home to lie down for a bit before heading in to get the patch, but I remembered that my husband had been asleep on the couch as I got the kids up and out of the house, and I really didn't want to run into him. So I made the judgement call that I would make it there. Mind over matter... or not.

Five minutes later and I was pulling into a small shopping center, where one can get a coffee, brake fluid, a pizza to bake at home, a pedicure or massage and pick up prescriptions all in one stop. I didn't choose any of the establishments. Instead, I headed for the farthest, emptiest corner, where I parked Bessy, climbed into the back and pulled out the bed (this is where having a camper van began to come in handy for unexpected reasons) and I laid down.

As I lay there, a million and one thoughts raced through my mind. How the fuck did I get here, lying in the back of my camper van in the parking lot of a mini strip mall on a Monday morning? How is it that I am again heading back to the hospital for another procedure and yet I don't feel I am any closer to understanding what the hell is going on with my body? Why am I going through all of this alone?

I set an alarm and I must have dozed off because I woke with a start, and realized that I had drool running down my chin. I immediately thought... what if someone has seen me? What if some of the other moms happened to swing by for their skinny soy lattes and had seen me "sleeping it off" in public, in broad daylight?! Oh the rumors that would run rampant. But I quickly realized that even if someone had seen me, and there are rumors, at least they would be a distraction away from whatever it is that is going on with my body. Maybe people will be so busy talking about me sleeping in my car that they won't notice the next time I pee myself in public or fall in the hallway of the school.

As I put Bessy into drive and pulled out of the parking lot, it crossed my mind, once again, "How the fuck did I get here?" I think that a lot these days.

I arrived at the hospital, and the pain was nearing defcon three as I stood in front of the reception desk, and tried to explain to the "kind" woman that I needed a spinal patch... now! Apparently "now" doesn't exist in this part of the hospital, because I was told to have a seat and informed that someone would call me shortly.

Shortly? What is shortly? Is it within sixty seconds? Five minutes? twenty, twenty-five... god forbid thirty minutes?! Because I had seconds before my head was going to explode, and there was nowhere to lie down, no couch, or even one of the silly double or triple type seats you often find in waiting rooms. Nowhere for me to get horizontal. Nowhere that would allow for the pain to stop. I slowly walked away from the kind woman and frantically searched for a place that would make the pain stop. And then I saw it. A place that I could lay down and get my body into a horizontal position. All I could think about was making the jackhammer in my head stop. I dropped to the floor off to the side of a row of chairs and laid down. That was where the nurse found me forty-five minutes later when they finally called my name.

Back in another backless gown (someone should really design something better than these things). Back in another hospital bed, and another gentle knock at the door. But instead of the abrupt entrance of "Poker Playing' doctor, it was a female doctor. She introduced herself and explained that she was the anesthesiologist that would be performing the spinal patch. She explained more about how my spinal fluid had been leaking out of my spine at the site of the injection. When I mentioned that I had the tap on Thursday, she expressed shock, but didn't tell me it's not possible (so take that, on-call doctor!).

The procedure itself was fairly quick and less painful (well at least not as long as the spinal tap). She drew blood from my arm, put a needle back in the exact same path that the first needle had traveled and injected my own blood into the area. As she pulled the needle out and snapped off her gloves, she explained that the blood would then clot up and block the leak. For an instant, I was struck with just how amazing the human body is and marveled at all it can do. But then I remembered that at the moment, I was in the hospital because my body had decided to not be amazing and not do marvelous things and I stopped thinking about the miracles of the human body and returned to just being pissed at my own.

The relief was instant. I didn't even have a twinge of a headache as I got dressed and leaned over to zip up my boots. It was gone! I instantly felt a great affinity for the doctor that had just left the room. She had been kind and caring. She had explained things clearly and in terms that I could understand. She had helped me, which is more than I can say for the "Poker Playing" doctor.

As I pulled onto the ramp and merged onto I-5, yet again on my way to pick up the kids from school, I was still thinking about the doctor I had met, and how much I had liked her. It struck me that I can do this! I can continue to go to appointments and procedures if that is what is needed to figure out what the hell is wrong with me. But I don't want to do it with doctors that don't seem to get me, that I don't click with and so as I pulled into the hell that is known as the pick-up line at school, I made another plan. A plan to return to my "Poker Playing" doctor to get the result of my spinal tap and to then go out and find another doctor. I may not be able to control what was happening with my body, but at least I could control who I choose to have around me as I try and figure it out.

Chapter Six

The Diagnosis—Not An "Oh Fuck" Moment

"At some point, you have to do what is right for you. Remember YOU matter and YOUR happiness is important."

It's Tuesday morning. I've recovered from my Thanksgiving day fall and I've spent the night thinking about my new resolve to find a doctor that I click with and avoid rolling onto my back because of the enormous and tender bruise left from yesterday morning's patch. I have just spent the past two hours volunteering in my youngest's classroom and I'm heading back to the hospital for an appointment with my "Poker Playing" doctor. He has the results from my MRI. He wants to discuss them. Little does he know that I have something to discuss as well...

Back in the office of the way-too-big-for-the-space desk, I glance around and I am pretty sure that there are more boxes and stacks of folders, files, pamphlets and books than there were the last time I sat in this seat. I wonder if my "Poker Playing" doctor has a hoarding problem.

As he settles into his seat and slips a floppy disk into his computer, I am thinking about how I am going to do this. How I am going to explain to him that although I appreciate all of his help, I really feel I need to find another doctor? Someone that I can bond with, someone that likes me and seems to care about me and what is going on with my body. Because that is what it comes down to. He strikes me as a stoic person, that doesn't have much of a personality, and although for some having a nice doctor might not matter, it does for me. I am a people person, and I want to be around other people persons. I want to feel like everyone likes me, and that includes my doctor.

I have been feeling a little bit better over the past few days (other than the whole headache thing). Both my feet seem to be not quite so "dead" and I haven't peed my pants in weeks! Initially he had told me that I have Transverse Myelitis. He said it was a temporary condition, that would go away in about a year. He said it would get better and it it seems that it is. Maybe the damn "Poker Playing" doctor has been right all along. Maybe I won't even need to find another doctor and I will be back to my "normal" self within a year. I can deal with that, no problem.

I am thinking all of this, as he clears his throat and begins to speak.

"I have the results of your spinal tap, and it is not Transverse Myelitis, and it is not temporary. You have Multiple Sclerosis."

I am not one to mince words, or hold back and my immediate response is, "Oh fuck!"

What "Poker Playing" doctor says next changes everything for me.

He leans back in his chair and calmly says, "No, this is not an "oh fuck" moment. This is a "oh damn" moment. There will be "oh fuck" moments, but this isn't one of them."

He then goes on to explain that although it might change my life and create moments of difficulty, that no one dies from MS. "If my five-year-old child was diagnosed with Leukemia, that is an "oh fuck" moment. My husband gets hit by a drunk driver and leaves me to raise eight kids on my own, that is an "oh fuck" moment. On a more global level, 9/11 was an "oh fuck" moment, but not this."

He takes a sip of something out of a mug resting on the too-big-for-the-space desk and goes on to tell me that the only thing that he feels bad about for me is having to tell people. He says that I strike him as a fairly independent person and he mentions that he has never seen me bring anyone to an appointment or procedure. I am somewhat surprised and touched to hear that he noticed. Perhaps my "Poker Playing" doctor does have a heart? Maybe he cares about me?

He says that in some ways, telling people that I have Multiple Sclerosis is like saying I have cancer, but not elaborating on what kind of cancer. Where and how severe it is. He explains that there are four different types of the disease and that it presents itself differently in every person. He warns me that just about everyone that I tell will know someone (or someone that knows someone else) that was diagnosed with MS. He advises me to be wary of the doomsday gloomers that will feel it necessary to mention their friend that had a cousin that was diagnosed at the age of nineteen and was in a wheelchair by the age of nineteen-and-a-half.

He looks solemnly but kindly at me and assures me that I am going to be okay.

He begins talking about some of his patients that were diagnosed during an initial exacerbation.

"What the fuck is that?!"

He tells me that they were then virtually symptom-free for many years after the first flare-up.

"Again, what the fuck is that?!?!"

As he continues to babble on, I find my mind floating back to the "oh

57

fuck" part of the conversation. If it isn't an "oh fuck" moment—if this isn't life shattering, then I can do it. I can figure it out and manage whatever comes down the road next. After all, it's an "oh damn" moment; no need to get in a tizzy over a harmless little word like "damn."

As I bring my mind back to the present and try to focus again on what he is saying, it occurs to me that he seems to be maintaining confidence that I will get through this "episode" and be back out running and living my "normal" life, soon.

Now I know that just mere minutes ago I was mentally drafting my break-up letter to my "Poker Playing" doctor, but something big has changed, my opinion of him, and his abilities and knowledge have been completely altered...

I take a big, shaky breath, determined that I am not going to cry. After all, this is only an "oh damn" moment and hardly worthy of shedding tears over—and certainly not in front of my "Poker Playing" doctor. Even if I am feeling a slight sense of affinity towards him.

I fear that he is going to think I am completely off my rocker when I ask, "Do I have to tell people?"

His answer is immediate, and said with a strong tone of confidence. "Not necessarily."

I think he is thrown by my follow-up question.

"Do I have to tell my husband?"

Chapter Seven

Coming Out:
How The World Found Out
I Was Damaged Goods

"Cry it all out. It is much better than keeping it all bottled up!"

As I sit in traffic on the strip of highway that connects I-5 and 520, I glance at the clock on the dashboard and see with growing panic that I am not going to make it to school before the bell rings. I won't be in the stupid pick-up line, waiting for my kids to run out and find me, and then vie for my attention as they share the good and the bad of their day at school. I realize that even though I am less than a mile from the school, the accident up ahead on the floating bridge is going to guarantee that I won't make it. It's only a mile and I still have ten minutes before the clanging erupts, but given that I have been at a complete standstill for the past fifteen minutes—shaded from the afternoon's unexpected sun by the tunnel—it doesn't look like I will be going anywhere anytime soon.

My mind starts racing. Who can I call to pick up the kids? Should I call the front office and ask that they be called there to wait until I can finally get off the damn highway and get there? My constant and chronic volunteering at the school ensures that everyone knows me and my three children. It also means that everyone knows that something has been going on with me medically over the past few months. They have seen me wobble, hobble and stumble when walking through the hallways. They know that I have had to cancel many of my weekly obligations in the classrooms because of doctor appointments. They know something is wrong with me, but they don't know that I have MS. The "Poker Playing" doctor and I are the only ones who know my fate and that I have a chronic illness. We are the only ones who know that this isn't going to go away. As I reach for my cell phone to try and sort out the kids until I can get there I think to myself, "I wonder if they know it's an "oh damn" moment."

I finally make it off of the freeway, through the Arboretum, where the late afternoon sun peeks through the tree-lined street, and to the school, where I climb the front steps and head to the main office to find my kids.

It's a busy afternoon, with three soccer practices at different times and on different fields, and it doesn't help that I am the coach of one of these practices. I realize that I am going to have to get my head in the game and stop repeating, "I have MS, I have MS" over and over again in my mind. I see people at the school, and at the practices, and I smile and make small talk, all the while thinking, "You don't know that I have MS." At some point during the afternoon I realize I don't want them to know. It all just seems way too personal and private to share.

The dinner mess has been cleared, homework tackled and the kids are bathed and ready for bed. As I tuck each one of them into bed, I try to imagine explaining to them what I learned today. How am I supposed to tell them about it when I don't really have a clue what it all means, and I certainly don't seem to have a clue what my body is going to do, day-to-day (or even it seems sometimes hour-to-hour)? I don't know what my future will look like. Maybe I will be like those patients my "Poker Playing" doctor mentioned. The ones that had a "flare-up" and then had few to no symptoms for long stretches of time. If that is the case, is it really worth telling the kids that it isn't temporary, that it isn't going away, that it will be in my body from now on?

Because that seems pretty fucking daunting to a seven-year-old mind. Is it worth it if I am going to be "pretty OK" in a few weeks or months? Do I want to instill that burden upon them? Do I want to tell them that their mommy is sick, that she has a disease? Because I am pretty sure "disease" is never going to be conceived as good thing by a child. It's a fucking scary word and my role in life is to protect my children from scary things.

As I hobble back downstairs and head for my husband's office, I take a deep breath and try to prepare myself for the conversation that is about to take place. He knows that I have had two MRI scans and a spinal tap and that I have gone in to get the results. When he asked me over dinner what had transpired, I had given him a slight shake of the head, with a look towards the kids (parent lingo for "not in front of the kids"). So, now that they are all tucked into their beds, drifting off into the world of dreams, I know that I have to go and talk to him.

I find that I am annoyed with him for asking. After all, he hasn't been to any of the appointments with me. He hasn't seemed overly concerned with what has been going on, so why does he now get to ask? I had asked the doctor that final question this morning for a reason. I am not sure that I want to tell him. But now that he has asked me directly, I can't lie. Sure, I might have been able to "withhold the information" but when confronted with the dead-on question, "what did the doctor say?", I can't avoid telling him. I also need to take the kids into account. It is going to affect them (how and to what degree, I have no way of knowing). But even if it is something that comes and goes, I am with them 24/7 and they are going to notice if mom is not running and playing with them, and I am pretty sure that they will notice if I pee my pants again.

I sit in a leather chair, tucked into the corner, beside the fireplace and start off with, "I have Multiple Sclerosis." His reaction is raw, and I believe genuine. I believe that he means it when he says he is so sorry to hear the news. He begins to ramble on about getting a second opinion, finding the best MS doctors in the area, looking into new treatments and medications and I find myself ready to boil over with anger. He is saying all the right words. He is suggesting the right ways to offer me help and support. But even though it has been a fairly quick diagnosis, he has not been there. He hasn't accompanied me to any of the appointments or procedures. He hasn't offered to help out with the kids. He hasn't talked to me about any of the things that have been going on and he certainly doesn't know how I feel about all of this. So he doesn't get to tell me to get a second opinion (maybe I now like my "Poker Playing" doctor) and he doesn't get to decide what I am going to do.

I feel as if I am talking to a stranger. Someone that doesn't know me, even though he has been my husband for the past twelve years and he is the father of my three children. It strikes me again that I don't want to tell strangers about this. I don't want to tell anyone, because maybe if I ignore it, it will just go away. After all, my "Poker Playing" doctor had said patients go into remission. If that happens, then I can just get my life back, move on and forget that any of this even happened.

Rather than address the anger that I am feeling, I decide to explain to my husband that I have not made a decision about what I am going to tell others (if anything.) I tell him the initial diagnosis of Transverse Myelitis is still out there, and I suggest that it can buy me time. I have explained to everyone that the doctor told me that it is a temporary condition, that will eventually go away. I told them that it could take up to a year or more for all the fluid on my spine to dry up and have my symptoms disappear and my thinking is... a year is a long time. A lot can happen in a year.

I explain to him that the doctor had told me about patients with MS that have an initial flare-up or two that then go into remission and don't have any significant issues for five or ten years. What if that could be me? If I get better, and stay that way? Is it really necessary to go through the whole pity/sympathy thing with people I know just casually through the kids' schools or from the neighborhood? Would it be better to just wait and see? Do I really want to label myself with a disease, "Oh there's Meg, she has MS" will surely become my tagline.

As I lay in bed my mind keeps returning to the thought that even if I have an incurable disease, it might be something that just shows up from time to time for a brief visit. Even if that is how it is going to pan out, and I am not going to end up in a wheelchair within thirty days, I can't stand the idea of not being honest with my kids. I can't imagine not telling them what I know (which isn't much.) I have always tried to be completely open and honest with them, and I know that now is not the time to make changes to that.

I wake in the morning a few minutes earlier than usual, and although the "dead feet" syndrome is on high alert, and the tightening around my ribs seems like it might legitimately squeeze me to death, I feel good. I slept well and I am now ready to talk to the kids about what the "Poker Playing" doctor told me yesterday. As they sit at the kitchen island, slurping the sugar-infused milk at the bottom of their cereal bowls, I hear Piper say, "well, if you think about it, you technically already were MS."

"Huh? What the what?!?!" I have just explained to them that I have a disease called Multiple Sclerosis, but that people call is MS for short. And this is my beautiful blonde beauty's response? And what does it mean anyway? I was already MS?"

In the exacerbated tone only a seven-year-old can pull off, she explains that my initials are MS—so I am already MS. Oh to be a seven-year-old girl.

I tell them as much as I know (which really isn't much). I tell them the story of the electrical cord and the lamp in the rain is still true. I tell them that sometimes my lamp will be left outside in the rain and the connections will be wonky and sometimes it will be kept inside, out of the rain, and the connections will work. I ask if they have any questions. Sam promptly says, "Yea, what time is soccer practice tonight?" Oh to be a nine-year-old boy.

Max's question is, "Can't we just get you a raincoat?" Oh to be a child of any age.

As I hear the thud of the sliding door, and reach out the window to wave goodbye to the kids, I am filled with a warm fuzzy feeling. I might have MS, and I might not know what the hell is going to happen, or what my future will look like, but I will have my kids with me, and that is all that really matters. The fact that I have just had a longer and more in depth conversation with my three young children than with my own husband is slightly alarming but then again, the kids have always had my back.

It's been a week since my last meeting with my "Poker Playing" doctor and the "heart-to-heart" conversation I had with my husband, about the diagnosis, and what (if anything) I am going to tell people. We have been invited to a Christmas party at one of his college buddy's homes. My folks are visiting and I think it will be good to get out and enjoy some holiday cheer. Although they have come for the holidays, and to help out, I don't really want to sit around just having them worry about me. Now that they know the full diagnosis (I called them after the "talk" with my husband, last week), I know that they want to do anything and everything they can to try and make things better for me. I think getting out and getting a bit drunk with them is just what the doctor would order.

The week flies by, with our days filled with holiday activities like baking cookies and wrapping presents and I am loving have my parents here. It's nice to have other adults to talk to. My husband and I never talk. We never argue, but we also never talk. Which is how I have managed to go the whole week without saying more than a few words to him. We haven't talked about the diagnosis. Not that I have wanted to talk to him about it, because I haven't. This seems far too personal to talk to about with someone that is in many ways a stranger to me. There are too many emotions wrapped up in those two words "incurable disease" to want to try and share any of it with him.

But now, tonight, I know I need to go and talk with him. The Christmas party is tomorrow night, and it will be the first time that he and I have been together in public since I was diagnosed. I want to set some boundaries.

I gently rap on the door to his office as I walk in and take up residency in the corner chair. As I curl my feet up underneath me to try and ward off a chill that has been lingering all night, it strikes me that it is sad that the only place that he and I speak these days, is here, in his office. Like it is some sort of "official appointment" taking place, rather than a married couple sharing their thoughts and feelings as they raise their family. Nope, not us, we meet in offices and have "serious talks." We haven't yet resorted to emailing each other, but I don't think it's that far off now that email is becoming "a thing."

I clear my throat before speaking, and realize how awkward I feel, talking about anything other than scheduling, bills or the kids with him. I start off, reiterating that I had not yet made my decision on how or what I am going to tell people about the MS. I ask that for the time being, we stick to the original Transverse Myelitis story that everyone already knows.

A sheepish look flashes across his face as he mumbles, "they already know." Anger slowly creeps in my direction, but I try to stay it with a question, "who already knows?" I figure that if we are just talking about the hosts of the party, the damage is minimal. Given that they are his close friends, it might be a forgivable offense. But his response is not what I am hoping for.

"They all know."

"All" consists of a large group that were friends in college. His friends. Although I am cordial to "all", I have never really felt accepted by this group. In their minds, he was a cradle-robber, marrying a woman almost nine years his junior. I have always had the sense that they think I chose him based on his financial situation. All of the money in world cannot make up fo the all consuming sense of sadness and loneliness I feel at the moment. I feel as if I have been betrayed by the one person that is supposed to stand by my side and have my back in life.

Anger arrives in full force, to accompany the hurt I feel deep within me. This is *my* disease! My information to share (or not share) and he has taken that away from me. I come to learn that he has spent the past week telling anyone and everyone that he had contact with, about my diagnosis. Subconsciously, I realize that this is how he has been "dealing" with it, coming to terms with having a spouse that is sick. But rather than coming to me to talk about it, he talked to others; anyone but me.

What he doesn't get, is that it is mine. That may sound selfish (or foolish) but I am the one who has it, who has to live with it, and all the symptoms that come along with it, and ultimately I am the one who should decide if and when people will know about it.

But the cat is out of the bag, and "not telling" is no longer an option. Knowing how voracious the grapevine is here in our city, I know that it will only be a matter of time before this information gets back to my close friends. If I continue on with my "Transverse Myelitis story", and then they hear the truth from others, it will be really fucking hard to explain how or why I had entrusted such personal information to social acquaintances and not to my true friends.

So, I come out! In a big way. Each and every time someone asks, "How are you?" or, "What happened to you?" (as I stumble, hobble and sometimes limp), I promptly explain that I have MS. I am telling the world that I have MS, one person at a time. I will grant you that this may have been a bit too much information for the gas attendant

I told yesterday, but I am quickly realizing that I am OK with people knowing. After all, if I look good, and tell them in a cheery way, maybe I can ward off the pity I so want to avoid. I work on being upbeat and peppy, so that they won't feel bad for me.

Any time someone reacts with, "gosh, I'm sorry" (which is a pretty normal response, it turns out) I quickly respond, "Please don't be! It's just something that is a part of my life. No worries." But what I am beginning to understand is that I have been so busy telling people that I am OK and emphatically declaring that it is just a "bump in the road." I have been so consumed with trying to prove to world that I am strong and that I can handle this to realize that my life as I knew it, is falling apart.

Chapter Eight

Jacked Up On Steroids

"There is a fine line between humor and despair.
Just make sure you are on the right side of that line!"

So, the world knows that I have MS and it has become a constant mantra in my head, the voice never ceasing to remind me that I have this stupid disease. Even if I were able to ignore it, my body is sure to chime in with wonky legs, fatigue or blurry vision. There is always something that reminds me: I am no longer the same. I am a different person. I put all of my energy towards trying to be "normal"—to continue all the things that I have always done and keep things the same. But the reality is that I am not "normal" anymore and nothing is the same.

We had a slight dusting of snow last night, nothing compared to what I am used to having grown up in New England, but the fact that most of Seattle is riddled with hills and most drivers in Seattle can't drive in snow, even a tiny bit can lead to the city shutting down. After starting the coffee-maker and grabbing a yogurt out of the fridge, I click on the morning news to see how "bad" it is out there in our version of a winter wonderland. Will the kids have a snow day? And if they do, what am I going to do with them? I have an appointment to go back and see my "Poker Playing" doctor. My symptoms have not improved (and actually seem to be worse) and I am eager to go to this appointment and find out why I am not getting better. I know he said it could take up to a year to recover from a flare-up, and I know that it has only been a few weeks, but I would think that there would be some improvement?!?!

Much to the kids' delight, school has been cancelled. Much to my delight, my friend Jules has said she can take the kids for the morning. Having dropped them off just a few minutes ago, I am headed north on I-5 for a visit with my doctor.

One of the very first things he asks me to do is to walk down to the end of the hall and back. Now, on any given day, without having a stupid disease that is messing with my legs and my walking, I don't think that I would enjoy walking up and down a hallway, knowing that someone is scrutinizing me. Add to this the fact that my gait has become very unsteady and I am wobbly as fuck; it is sheer misery! But apparently I nailed it because he announces, "Great!! (with actual enthusiasm?!?) and invites me back into his office.

"I think you need to do a round of steroids."

Huh? What? I mean I am all about exercising and I most certainly take some pride in my decent muscle tone but immediately think, "no thanks; those things can mess you up."

He explains that it is common to use Solu Medrol as a means to try and help speed up the recovery of an exacerbation. Since my symptoms have not improved, I am willing to hear him out on this one. Apparently, it is not an immediate fix, but it will help dry up the fluid in my spinal cord a bit faster.

"If you took two of yourself and one had the steroids and the other didn't, in a year, both of you might be fine, but the you that got the steroids would have recovered faster."

"Huh, two of me?" I have a bit of trouble trying to drag my mind away from the idea of there being two of me. Imagine all the shit that I could get done if there were two of me doing things... Eventually I shake this from my mind and tell my "Poker Playing" doctor that I am in. I ask what I need to do next.

He seems surprised that I have agreed. "First, you will have to be in the hospital for three days."

Okay, I'm out! Does he not understand that I've got three kids and a busy life? I can't be in the hospital for three days! Hell, I have never spent even one night away from my kids. Three is definitely out of the question! I haven't said this out loud, and realize that he hasn't stopped talking. Focusing on his words, I hear him explaining that it involves having two infusions a day, at least four hours apart.

Two infusions? Four hours apart? How long are the damn infusions? I suck at math but even if they are super long, there are still a lot of hours in a day. Hours that I could be home with my children, doing all the things that I need to be doing. When I hear that it only takes an hour for each infusion I ask what I will be doing between the two. When he tells me nothing really, I jump at the chance to ask, could I leave in between? Could I simply come in the morning, after dropping the kids off at school to get my first infusion, then leave to do all my "mommy-ing" things, come back four hours later to be hooked up for round two of the day?

He said it sounded like a plan, but that I would still need to spend my nights in the hospital.

Why? I immediately wonder what is going to happen to me? Are there some horrible, terrible, no-good side effects to these steroids that he is failing to mention?

When he tells me that the main reason for staying in the hospital is that the steroids make it difficult to sleep, and they can give me something to help me fall asleep, I assure him that sleep has never been a high priority for me and it seems like a crazy stupid reason to have to stay in the hospital. I also tell him that I am pretty sure a few shots of whiskey would do the trick, if needed.

He doesn't look very happy with me. I get the sense this is not the way he anticipated this conversation going and I am pretty sure he didn't care for my attempt at humor with the whiskey joke. He stands, makes his way around the way-too-big-for-the-space desk and opens the office door. Just before stepping into the hallway (formerly my racetrack for walking) he says he will check with the office manager about my proposal. As I reach down to put my boots back on, he tells me he should have an answer by the end of the day, and promises me that he will give me a call. As he shuts the door, I hear him say, "I'm sure you will be in Target."

Oh look at Mr. Dr. McFunny! Is this a personality I am seeing? Did I just see a smile curl the side of his mouth? Maybe my "Poker Playing" doctor isn't so bad, maybe he does "get me?" What I thought, but didn't say, was that given that Christmas is less than a week away, there is a damn good chance that I might be in Target when he calls, after all, I am here and I have things I have to do.

When the doctor calls me (I am not in Target), I learn that protocol has changed since he last had a patient with MS. A hospital stay is no longer required (or allowed by insurance companies). Apparently they feel as I do, which is that staying overnight during three days of steroids is bullshit.

As I sit on hold, waiting for the scheduling nurse to answer, I immediately think about the kids and their schedules. From the beginning of all of this, I have worked very hard to try and not let what is going on with me medically affect my role as their mom. I have always been the one to get them up in morning. I am the one that gets breakfast into their bellies, lunches made, backpacks ready. I am the one that drops them off at school and I am the one that is there at the end of each day, ready to whisk them off to soccer practice or a playdate and then home for dinner, homework, baths and bed. It is what I do and I will be damned if that is going to change just because of some stupid disease.

I spent a little bit of time over the past few weeks searching the internet for information about Multiple Sclerosis and I found a few blogs that caught my attention. I read somewhere, "I may have MS, but it doesn't have me" and I grabbed onto that notion—I'll be damned if I am going to let this change me or mess with my kids' lives.

I am pretty sure the scheduling nurse thinks I am a complete wacko—as I explain that I drop my kids off at school at 8:30 a.m., the drive takes me thirty minutes, so my first infusion of the day will need to be at 9. When she responded with, "OK, so 9:30?" I may have barked "No! I need 9 because I need to be done by 10, so that I can come back at 2, done by 2:45. I realized that I would be late for pick-up, but it would be close enough that my kids could just wait with a friend or in the office until I made it there.

Conceivably, this could have worked, but what I didn't take into calculation is the time it would take to check in and for the nurses to order my medicine down from the pharmacy (apparently they won't put an order in until a patient has actually arrived). Everyone at the infusion center is wonderful and kind and caring. But their average patient is 70+ years old. There are a shit ton of retirement communities in the blocks surrounding the hospital, so it makes sense. Generally, their patients have very few time constraints and view a visit to the infusion center as the day's outing! An event! I am a new entity to them. Young, vibrant, and in a hurry!

As I stand at the check-in desk waiting for the nurse behind a computer to finish up with a phone call, I glance around at my surroundings. Each time I head off for a new procedure, in a new facility, I struggle with trying to stay calm. I try to not panic. I try not to let the thoughts about "what will my life look like?" consume me. Things like "am I going to end up alone and in a wheelchair?" really freak me out. It is hard, because being here, having to endure more medical procedures just reminds me that this is all real. It's not just some bad dream and I am not going to wake up to discover that I don't have this fucking disease, that I can still go for my beloved runs, that I am in a happy marriage. None of that is going to happen, because this is real and it is scary as shit!

The nurse hangs up the phone and asks which patient I am here to visit with or who I am picking up. See, I don't look like there is anything wrong with me!

I explain that I am here for an infusion. She doesn't seem to believe me. As she begins to look for my file, (I'm pretty sure she doesn't think it will be there) another nurse approaches, introduces herself as "Robin" and invites me into the infusion room.

It is one of the blandest, most hospital-like rooms I have ever seen. It's a fairly small room painted a pale and putrid shade of green. Around the perimeter, there are large drab gray barco-loungers, a few plastic chairs and four TVs that look like they are left over from the 90s, hanging from various places on the walls. There are four patients, already hooked up, medicine finding its way into their veins. Other than the nurse standing by my side, I am the youngest one in the room by at least twenty-five years.

It is a room full of old people. Because old people have medical problems. Old people have bodies that have begun to peter out, not functioning as they once did. Old people need medicine. Not young mothers that are fit and active and too busy to just sit around to wait for the drugs to do their job. I feel panic begin to well up in my chest.

I don't want to be here!!! I don't belong here!!! I don't want to have MS!!!! I don't deserve to have this disease!!! What did I do wrong??

Robin shows me to one of the two remaining barco-loungers, shows me where I can hang my coat and scarf and says she is going to get my medicine. As I plop down onto the cracked pleather of the infusion chair, I grab my phone out of my bag and turn it to silent mode. I then grab my headphones and iPod, hoping that listening to some music might help to calm the panic that is still lying just below the surface.

I have been waiting for about ten minutes (I am obviously not going to be able to stick to the schedule) when a woman enters the room, and immediately approaches me. Before I even have time to take my earbuds out or turn my music down, she is saying something and making large hand gestures at me. As her words reach me through the music, I realize that she is telling me that "these" chairs are for patients only and she is telling me that I have to move to one of the pathetically sad plastic chairs that are strewn haphazardly throughout the space. I pull out my earbuds and hear her demand, "You need to move, you are in my mother's seat."

I feel stupid. I feel as if I have done something wrong. I feel embarrassed. Here is this lady telling me exactly what I have been trying to say for weeks—I don't belong here. I don't look like there is anything wrong with me. I am in the wrong place, living the wrong life. As I stand up, smoothing down the front of my pink corduroy skirt, I wrap the ends of my gray cashmere sweater around my body as if to protect me from her accusations.

I am not sure what I am about to say, but it is probably a good thing that Robin reappears at this exact moment, waving a three-ring binder with my name and picture on the front singing out, "ok well now, you are all set, your meds will be sent down in about thirty minutes and then we can get you started."

Thirty minutes? My schedule is fucked! I am going to have to come up with Plan B for getting the kids after school and having infusion number two done.

77

I glance at the woman, who, moments ago acted like she was ready to jump me over being in her "mother's seat." She has seen my picture on the front of the binder and she has heard what Robin just said. I want to raise my hands and yell out, "Bam, Bitch! Who doesn't belong here now?" but given where we are and my current audience of octogenarians, I think better of it. I simply smile (I like to think demurely) as I settle back down in my seat.

It is 10:15 by the time Robin returns with a bag of liquid and an infusion pole. I have managed to work myself up into a totally tizzy, worrying about the schedule and getting my kids. I have to be there, it is what I do and I don't want things to be different. They can't be, because then it means that this stupid disease is winning.

I explain to Robin that I have three kids and that I am trying to make sure that I am there to pick them up at the end of the day. As the words are coming out of my mouth, I am aware that I may well sound borderline bat shit crazy. As if there is no one else on the entire planet that could pick my kids up from school, that could help me out by watching them, because I have some major medical issues going on right now and need to be here in the hospital trying to get better. I know it sounds like I'm nuts, and I'm am sure that Robin is judging me as a high strung, overly pushy bitch until she leans in and gives me a huge hug and whispers in my ear, "honey, I have two babies of my own at home and I completely get it. I will do everything I can to help you make the schedule work and make sure that you are there when the bell rings."

Well shit—cue the waterworks. Here is someone that gets it! Gets me! She seems to really understand that it is so much more than just making it back to their school before the bell and she wants to try and help me. I have been so wrapped up in trying to keep appearances up, in trying to show the world that I am strong and that I can handle whatever shit this disease decides to dish out. I have been so opposed to having anyone feel pity for me, that I have forgotten that there are plenty of people out there who want to help, who empathize with what I have been going through. I just have to remember to let them in; to let them help.

As I wipe the tears from my eyes and settle back down in the chair, I lie my arm on the movable tray that is attached to the chair and wait for Robin to stick the IV needle into my arm. After a brief discussion about my preferred location of the port, we decide that my left forearm would be best and she has the line in and the juices flowing in no time flat.

"When were you diagnosed, honey?"

To have someone that appears to be ten years my junior call me honey would normally make my skin crawl. I am just not a touchy, mushy type of person. But for some reason, Robin saying it doesn't bother me in the least. It actually feels nice to have someone use a term of endearment—it's been a long time since my husband has used any. It's nice to feel cared about.

We chat for a bit about "how I knew something was wrong"—I tell her given what I have been experiencing, it would be hard to not know. We talk about the kids and their ages and she suggests that I just bring them back with me for my second infusion of the day. That way I will be able to pick them up—be there like I always am—and then come back for round two. I'm not crazy about the idea of bringing the kids here—as I said, it's pretty gloomy and there isn't a whole lot of room. I sure as hell don't want one of them to be sitting in that lady's mother's seat in the off chance that she is coming back later today too. But I don't really have any other alternative so once Robin disconnects me from the IV bag and wraps the port with a gauze sleeve, I head back to the car to go get my kids.

They seem excited, curious and a bit apprehensive when I tell them that we are going on a "field trip" to the hospital so that mommy can get her medicine. I think they have been curious about what I have been doing on these days when I frantically speed off to the hospital after drop-off. I know that they are curious about the gauze sleeve around my arm and the needle that is lurking beneath. Maybe it makes me cool that I have a needle stuck in my arm?

I believe in distraction. I believe in bribery. These are two of the things that make me such a good mother—and so a quick run through the drive-thru of McDonald's and all three kids are ready and rarin' to go! We are off the infusion room! Yippee!!!!

Round two is much faster. Robin is there, ready and waiting—drugs and lollipops in hand. God I love this woman—and what is a bit more sugar on top of the crap I just fed them? I let out a small sigh of relief when I see that only one other chair is occupied—fewer old people for my kids to annoy. I admit, I am completely relieved to not see the lady from this morning, or her mother. The kids have a bunch of questions for me, about the needle (did it hurt?) about the medicine (what does it do?) and about my legs (how are they feeling?).

As Max climbs up into my lap, and Sam and Piper slink to the ground at my feet, using my legs to prop themselves up, I am filled with an enormous sense that everything is going to be OK. That no matter what, these three little people are on my team, and that together, with them, I am going to be OK.

I am glad that Robin suggested that I bring them here because it is important for them to know what it is that I am going through. It is good for them to be able to envision where it is I am running off to and it is good to sit and let them just talk about the disease, and to ask questions. Having them here, I am no longer obsessing about the disease, I am focused on them, and making sure that they are alright and that seems like the old me, the "normal" me, the me I was before I was told I have MS.

We manage to make it home by 6 and after a quick dinner of fish sticks and mac 'n cheese, homework and baths, I curl up with the kids in the boys' room and read them a bunch of books. More than likely, they would be happy with just one or two, but I am completely wrapped up in cuddling with them and just enjoying being with them that I pull book after book off the shelf.

As I pull the door shut to Piper's room, having just tucked her in, I reach down to pick up the damp towel laying at my feet in middle of the hallway and it strikes me that I am not tired. I am not feeling the overwhelming fatigue that has haunted me over the past few months. I don't feel as if I am going to die if I don't get in bed immediately. Actually, I feel pretty good. I feel as if I can go down and tackle the pile of laundry that has taken over the garage since I got "sick."

I spend the entire night being a whirling dervish. By the time I am ready to wake the kids up, every surface in the house has been cleaned, all the laundry is done, the kids' lunches (way more gourmet than usual) are packed, and the garage has been vacuumed out—it is the only place that I could vacuum in middle of the night without fear of waking up the kids! I love steroids.

Day two of the infusions goes off without a hitch. Robin is ready and waiting with my meds when I walk into the infusion center at 9:15 sharp, I make it back for number two right at 2:00 and am on the road headed to get the kids by 2:35. I spend the night cleaning again, but this time, a little less enthusiastically. I am exhausted, but I am also completely jacked up—it's almost like I can feel the steroids flowing through my veins, and I can only hope that they are doing what they are supposed to, and helping me get better.

Day three, I am just done. Fried. Edgy. Jittery. Not good feelings, but I get the kids up and off to school, and hit the road. I arrive, but Robin is not there. Instead, Pat is at the desk, she has my binder and meds in hand and smiles when I give her my name.

"I've heard about you, and your beautiful kids. Robin had to take the day off, one of her kids wasn't feeling well, but she has filled me in on you and your hectic schedule. I promise, I will do my best to make sure we stick to it and get you out of here ASAP."

Again, the damn waterworks. These people don't know me, they don't owe me anything, and yet here they are, helping me try and to continue to be me throughout all of this. Granted it may well just be the lack of sleep that has led to this round of tears, but I am so moved by their kindness. I don't really know how to say thank you in a way that will express just how much it means to me. Knowing that there are people out there, willing to care for me, to help me, leaves me feeling vulnerable, but in some strange way, I am OK with it.

I try and sleep but the steroids don't seem to think that it is a good idea. They are still running through my body, hopefully making things better. So I build a fire to ward off the dampness the rain has brought on and spend the night curled up in a chair, reading. I read an entire book and then I get up, make the kids' lunches, wake them up and drive them to school. I walk back in the house, walk straight up the stairs and climb into bed. I set my alarm for 2:30, so that I can be at pick-up at 3:05 and I fall into a deep and much needed sleep without thinking about MS even once.

Chapter Nine

Breaking Up Is Hard to Do

"You will be fine. You know, canes make people look distinguished. You just have to talk with an accent and only use Gray Poupon from now on."

It's now early May and I am once again back in my "Poker Playing" doctor's office. As I wait for him to return from an "urgent call" he had to take, I sit and think about the past few months.

I have spent them buried up to my eyeballs in anything and everything auction related. Against my husband's wishes, I made the decision to continue my role as the auction chair for the kids' public elementary school. I have done it before and I am well aware of the amount of time and energy it takes and I even remember saying, "remind me to never do that again" when the last one came to an end. The steroids did their thing, and I have been feeling better. Not "I'm great" better, but there have been improvements. The dead-feet only seems to visit at night, after a long day out and about with the kids. The annoying and scary tightening around my ribs has gone away, and I definitely feel as if my energy level is on the rise!

From the start of this all, I kept thinking to myself, "ok, so I have this disease but that doesn't mean that I have to change because of it." I don't want MS (this new label I have in life) to define who I am or what I can do. At least not now, when I still seem to have some control over things. Maybe later, in the future, I will have to make concessions—change the way I do things, or accept that there are things that I can no longer do. But for now, I need to try and get back to normal.

So I agreed to do the auction, because that seemed "normal." And things got better for a little bit. It was crazy hectic, and I may have overdone it on a few occasions and climbed into bed at the end of the day on legs that could no longer support me, but the MS shit was better. I didn't have time to sit around and think about this stupid disease. There isn't space in my brain for the constant "I have MS, I have MS" chant that has been on autoplay since the shit started to go down last spring and I enjoyed the break from constantly thinking about the disease and what it was doing to my body.

Being a part of the auction forced me to get out of the house, and to continue to be out and about interacting with people. It also forced me to become more comfortable with people knowing about my diagnosis. If people were going to know, I would much prefer that it is simply just another "thing" about me, rather than it being "the" thing.

I let out a small laugh when I think of my friend and co-chair Bob, and how much he has helped me learn to accept this new thing in my life. How he has embraced the humor that I am quickly learning I need in order to not let all this get me down. At one of our weekly meetings, Bob and I had spread out our respective files and papers and as we waited for the 20+ parents to grab a coffee and find a seat, he yelled out to me from the other side of the room.

"Hey, MS!" He has the "endearing" habit of calling people by their initials and as my daughter had pointed out months ago, when I told her about my diagnosis, mine are M.S.

This was followed by an audible hush. Everyone in the room had stopped talking and was now looking from me to Bob and back again.

A woman standing next to him stage whispered, "Bob! She has MS!" Bob's response to this was, "Uh, I think she knows that!" Moments like that, reasons to laugh, are what have helped me get through the past few months. That, and the steroids did seem to be help. It wasn't an immediate improvement, not like I went to bed and woke up the next morning all better, but slowly it had gotten better.

I had made it through the auction, running around like a chicken with its head cut off, making sure the evening ran smoothly. I made it through the final week leading up to the event with very little sleep. I managed to be on my feet for hours on the day of the event and I still made it up on to the stage, unassisted, in high heels at the end of the evening. As I stood there next to Bob, in front of the entire community to accept their gift of gratitude for our time and effort, he leaned over and whispered, "doesn't look like there is anything wrong with you, hot momma."

That was last week, and yet again, a lot has changed in a short period of time. I can't even imagine trying to wear those heels right now. As it is, I had to use the wall to balance myself as I walked down the dreaded hallway leading to the doctor's office. It had been so amazing, so special, so normal, and now it seems to be slipping away again!

As he enters the room, my "Poker Playing" doctor is carrying a fairly large stack of "stuff." It's a random assortment of things. There are a few colorful pamphlets, a DVD, a t-shirt, a mug and even a frisbee. He dumps them in my lap.

This is my introduction into the world of "Disease Modifying Drugs" (often referred to as DMDs, according to him). He explains that he doesn't usually see patients with MS. He says he is more of a Carpal Tunnel Syndrome type of guy, and I'm not sure what to say to that, so I just smile and nod. He explains that being located in an area that has higher numbers of people with the disease, he often has pharmaceutical reps stop by with "educational materials" pertaining to their

MS drugs. He has not had a reason to use them. I am now his reason. I, again, smile and nod. I'm quieter than I have been in the past, and he picks up on this.

He asks about me, about how I have been feeling and I'll be damned if the fucking waterworks decide to pop in for a visit. I am an emotional wreck lately; I can't seem to keep it all together and I am mortified to be sitting here in front of him, as my tears begin to soak the pile of crap he dumped in my lap.

He stands and comes out from behind the too-big-for-the-space desk, pulls a handkerchief out of his pocket and hands it to me. I am sitting here bawling my eyes out, teetering on the brink of a break down and the only thing I can think is, "a handkerchief???? Really???" I mean maybe if he was a 75-year-old man. But as I've said, he is my age. Who, at our age, carries around a handkerchief? Plus isn't it really unsanitary? Am I supposed to blow my snot into it, smear my now destroyed mascara all over it, and then hand it back? What does one do in this situation?

The good news is that all of this thinking about the handkerchief makes me stop feeling sorry for myself and it stops the waterworks. Who knows, maybe my "Poker Playing" doctor is that good, that he knew that just the sight of his handkerchief would stop the tears. Maybe he knew that he wouldn't actually need to hand it over to me for it to be effective. Maybe? Or maybe he is just an odd duck that does odd things. But whatever the case...

I have been thinking that maybe I should seek a second opinion. Even though my opinion of him and his skills as a doctor and his demeanor as a human being have changed drastically over the past few months, I am still not sure he knows what he is doing, and I am not sure that I believe everything that he says. That seems pretty huge to me. Those are things that are definitely important. I am extremely thankful to him for everything he has done thus far, and for his amazing words of wisdom that helped shaped even my initial reaction to being diagnosed but, is he the right doctor for me? The one that will be best for me and my new journey into a life living with a chronic disease. If not, how the hell do I tell him this? How do I break up with him and set out to find the "right" one?

Once again, my "Poker Playing" doctor surprises me with what he says next, having returned to his chair behind the too-big-for-the-space desk.

"I think you need to get a second opinion. I think you need to find a neurologist that specializes in Multiple Sclerosis."

Yes! He is suggesting exactly what I have been thinking. He is saving me from having to worry about breaking up with him!

But then I think. "Wait, does that mean he is breaking up with me? Am I the dumpee? And if so, why? Why wouldn't he want me as a patient? I have been kind and polite and occasionally humorous." What is wrong with me?

Here he is, giving me an out, exactly what I have been thinking would be best for me, and here I am concerned that maybe he doesn't like me. What the fuck is wrong with me!?

He has written down the names and phone numbers of a few well known MS doctors in our area and reaches across the too-big-for-the-space desk. As I gather all the drug swag he had dumped in my lap, I reach out to grab the slip of paper. It is just like a break-up, and I don't know what to say.

He tells me he thinks that Dr. L. at the University of Washington MS clinic would be a good fit and asks if I would like him to make a call to get me in to see her. I say I would appreciate it. As I gather up my belongings, I scramble to find something more to say. How do I thank someone for being the one to inform me that I have a chronic illness? How do I thank him for putting up with my stubborness?

How do I thank him for showing me kindness, even if it was in the form of a questionable handkerchief? How do I thank him for playing poker with me? I reach out to shake his hand and say, "thank you, for everything. If I ever meet someone with Carpal Tunnel Syndrome, I will be sure to recommend you." And on that note, I walk out of his office, and out of his life.

I call Dr. L.'s office from the car and I make an appointment for next week. As I put Bessy into reverse and back out of my parking space, I realize that I feel like crap. I am exhausted and all I want to do is go home and curl up in bed. Ignoring this stupid disease is getting harder and harder. It just seems to constantly remind me that I am no longer "normal."

Per usual, with all the kids' school work, activities and playdates, the week flies by. I have my first appointment with Dr. L. this morning and as I pull into the parking garage, just fifteen minutes after dropping the kids off at school, I am appreciative of the more convenient location. I'm feeling nervous and a bit excited. I'm not sure why. Maybe my "Poker Playing" doctor had it all wrong and it isn't actually Multiple Sclerosis. Maybe all of this shit will just go away?

There is a restored sense of hope. Maybe all of this is just a huge mistake and maybe I am going to be just fine, back to normal in no time. It seems that getting a new doctor has allowed me to think that maybe I don't have MS, that this isn't as serious as my "Poker Playing" doctor had made it out to be.

I am shown into an exam room and have been waiting for a few minutes when there is a light knock on the door. In walks a woman that is another mom at my children's school. I am sure that the look on my face clearly reads, "what the fuck?!?" Although I don't know what she does, I do know that she is not a doctor and I wonder what the hell she is doing, standing in my exam room. She is someone I consider a friend, but not someone that I would invite to accompany me... anywhere, let alone this appointment. Hell, I have never invited anyone to accompany me. Well, anyone but my husband. Suffice to say I have never had someone else at an appointment with me.

It turns out, she is the medical research director for Dr. L. and although she heard through the grapevine that I was recently diagnosed with MS and she had seen my name on the doctor's schedule, she had not approached me before my appointment out of respect for patient confidentiality and not knowing if I was comfortable openly talking about my recent diagnosis.

I immediately flash back to the auction meeting, to Bob calling me MS, to everyone in the room turning to look at me. I hear the mock whisper, "she has MS." She was standing just feet away from me. She could have said something then? It strikes me as a bit odd, and I feel a bit like I have been ambushed, but that doesn't last for long.

Having her here, and listening to her ringing endorsement for Dr. L. makes the appointment and my decision on a new doctor a lot easier, but it also starts my relationship with the doctor on a level beyond just being another patient of hers. I feel as if she is my friend, and for me and my personality, that is exactly what I need. Someone I like and that likes me too. The fact that she is a brilliant woman heavily invested in her patients' care and highly respected nationally for her work within the MS research community all make my decision a solid one, but it really boils down to liking one another.

As I walk out of the building and head for the parking garage, I try and shield yet another pile of DMD paraphernalia from the deluge that is falling from the early afternoon sky. I am feeling optimistic about my new doctor, my diagnosis, and my future. I think to myself, "with people like that on my team, how can I not win over this thing?"

Chapter Ten

Shooting Up An Orange

"Just keep thinking about pizza. Good pizza—East coast pizza!
Oh, and think about friends. Good friends—East coast friends.
But really, think about pizza. It makes EVERYTHING
better!"

Before leaving the appointment, we had discussed the different DMDs that are available. She had explained to me that there are three different drugs; all three are interferons, and all three involve giving myself an injection. All of them sound pretty shitty to me. Never in my life would I have thought that I would be sticking myself with a needle. To be honest, I still don't, which might be a problem, since I am currently sitting in my kitchen, waiting for a nurse to arrive and teach me how to stick a needle in my body. Good times.

It's been two weeks since I met Dr. L. I've been back to the infusion center for another round of steroids and the symptoms seem to be improving again. Fingers crossed that it lasts this time. I don't mind the steroids, particularly since they seem to help, but they do leave me feeling jittery and a bit "off" for a few days. This time around, there was a second step, once I had completed my three days of infusions, Dr. L. prescribed a Prednisone pack—oral steroids, to help taper me off. It seemed to help a little bit with the icky feelings, but I'm not sure I've noticed a huge difference.

I didn't get much sleep last night. My mind kept returning to the idea that I was now going to be self-injecting a drug into my body once a week. Logically, I know that people do it. I know people with diabetes that have to do it all the time. I get that. I just don't think that I am one of them. I don't know if I can do it.

When nurse Mary had called to schedule the appointment, she had asked if I would be the one doing the injections. This caught me a bit off guard—I didn't realize that I had options? Maybe I wouldn't have to be the one to stick a needle in my body weekly?!?! This was news to me and I began to feel a bit more optimistic. Until she suggested that perhaps my spouse would be the one to administer my medication. That stopped that line of thought. There is no way that my husband would be willing or able to participate in this. On top of being incredibly squeamish about needles, he hasn't played an active role in my life with this disease up until this point and I have no reason to think that is going to change. So, unless I decide that one of the kids is a budding nurse with a desire to poke mommy with a sharp object, it looks like I will be sticking myself with a needle. I just hope it doesn't have to be my ass, as I think that would be awkward and hard to do. These are the things that flew around my mind all night long.

The doorbell rings, snapping me out of my semi-conscious state on the couch, and I go to meet Mary, my traveling nurse. As she spreads her supplies out on the kitchen table, I see an orange, needles, some gauze and medical tape and a small bottle filled with a liquid. I am assuming this is the medicine, and the needles make sense, but I am not sure what to make of the orange... do I need to eat before shooting myself up? Did she think I might get hungry during this appointment? Did she think she was going to get hungry? And there is another thing that grabs my attention—a bottle of laundry detergent?!?! The only thing I can think is, "I am going to stick myself with a needle... it will bleed... it might get on my clothing, or her clothing, and so she has come prepared to wash my laundry?!?! It seems a bit odd and out of place for a traveling nurse, but whatever. To each his own.

Mary begins by showing me the needles and the packaging that they come in. She, then, goes into detail about disposing of the needles—and this is where the laundry detergent begins to make sense. "It is the bottle itself, not what it once contained, that is important. It is a safe receptacle for my used needles!" She suggests that I clearly label it with "Rx" and keep it out of reach from the kids. Ya think? She tells me that I will need to check with my city waste and disposal procedures to find out where I can dispose of the bottle of needles, once it is full. I look at the size of her jug, I look at the size of the needles and I think to myself, "yea, it's going to be about fifteen years before I fill one of those suckers up, so I will deal with the city at a later date…"

Mary then picks up the orange and begins to explain that with Avonex, the injections are inserted directly into a muscle, allowing for the drug to enter the bloodstream as quickly as possible. She says that they use an orange to practice on because the skin of an orange is very similar in resistance to human skin and is a perfect practice method for learning to inject someone. My mind flits to, "I wonder how many drug users have used an orange to practice their injection skills—pretty sure that number is low."

Focusing back in on Mary, I realize that she is holding a needle and the orange out to me. I hold the orange in my left hand and plunge the needle. Not surprisingly, I have no problems with shooting up that poor defenseless orange. None whatsoever! I may have stabbed it more times than was actually necessary but it was somewhat therapeutic, like I was taking my anger, frustration, sadness, and worry out on this innocent piece of fruit. What had it ever done to me?

As Mary reached to gently remove the orange from my clenched hand, I realize I may have alarmed her with my enthusiasm to inflict pain upon a garden variety piece of fruit! Oops. It was super easy to push the needle into the orange, but when Mary announces that it is time for me to administer my first dose of the medicine, it's a completely different story! I am scared shitless. I don't want to do this!!!!

I have been listening carefully throughout Mary's demonstration and instructions, and beyond taking great enjoyment in inflicting harm on a piece of fruit, I have spent the past thirty minutes trying to mentally prepare myself for this. "No problem!" "It's not something that I have ever wanted to do, but then again, I never wanted MS... it is what it is... no big deal!" I try telling myself to just suck it up, and remind myself that there are plenty of people with far worse situations than mine.

I look at my watch, and tell myself I have ten minutes to get this done. I remind myself that I have a yoga class that starts in less than an hour, and I'll be damned if I am going to miss it because I am too busy fucking around with oranges and needles!

I take the needle in my hand, pull the skin on my thigh taut, just as Mary has shown me, and I freeze! I try to talk myself into it and even say out loud, "okay, this time, one... two... three!" And... nothing! One... two... three! One... two... three!!! This goes on for about forty minutes (no yoga for me) and I am surprised to find myself in tears.

As much as I want to just do it, I find I can't. There is something about my mind, wanting to instinctively protect my body... as in, "Hell No! I am not going to let you jam that needle into your own leg! That is just stupid!" I am mad and frustrated with myself. Mary is kind, patient and supportive, and eventually I do manage to give myself the shot, but it takes well over an hour of me sitting here with the needle hovering over my thigh, before I finally built up the courage to do it.

Truth be told, it isn't as bad as I had imagined, but it was not pleasant either. Injecting directly into the muscle is painful. Jabbing a needle into you body is painful. Plain and simple. But I did it, and as I help Mary pack up her stuff, I can't help but feel a little bit proud of myself. I honestly didn't think I would be able to do it, but I did! I've missed my yoga class but that's OK, I figure grabbing a nap before heading out to get the kids is a good idea.

One of the things that Mary mentioned is that there might be side effects that come with using the interferons. I read over the pamphlet she left while trying to fall asleep for a nap. It says that some people experience flu-like symptoms and I wonder if I will be one of the "lucky" ones that have these reactions.

I get my answer just a few hours later as I sit on the bathroom floor, in pajamas drenched with my sweat, hugging the toilet and puking my brains out. Flu-like symptoms—check! It is a long ass night and I am exhausted when the alarm goes off at 6 and I get up to get the kids ready for school. The vomiting had lasted until about 3 in the morning, and although I feel like the walking dead, there is nothing left in my stomach to purge and the profuse sweating had stopped sometime in the early morning hours.

I drop the kids off at school and head to the gym for my workout. I then go home and climb back in bed, where I stay until it is time to get the kids from school and get them off to soccer practices and home for dinner. By dinner time, all the flu-like symptoms have subsided and I am actually feeling fairly good. I know that I need to pick a night of the week to give myself the shot and I've thought about it a lot today. I have decided to do it on Sunday nights. I figure, if I know that I will have a long night, but can still get up and get the kids to school and then hit the gym to try and sweat out the icky feeling then I will have the rest of the week to feel better. I remind myself that this is just another hurdle on my road to feeling better and getting my life back on track.

The week is fairly uneventful, the symptoms seem to be quieting down and although I begin to feel anxious when the weekend arrives, I am feeling full of confidence when I announce to the kids on Sunday afternoon that, "mommy needs to go give herself the medicine" and I head up to the bedroom. I may have been a bit cocky about it though. After sitting on the chair in the corner, with the needle prone to go into my thigh for over 30 minutes, I head back downstairs, pour myself a large glass of wine and head back up to try again. This time it only takes fifteen minutes for me to muster up the nerve to sink the needle into my leg and then I head back down to finish dinner and start getting the kids ready for school tomorrow. I am on the road to recovery. I am taking steps to fight this disease and I am feeling good about my decision to start the DMD.

Chapter Eleven

Segway Into My New Life

"As far as the stairs and falling, I'll tell you what I tell my girls:
Hold onto the fucking railing—it's what it's there for!"

I've now been shooting up on Avonex once a week for about six months. Truthfully, it hasn't gotten any easier to jam a needle into my thigh and I continue to spend my Sunday nights on the bathroom floor, often times hugging the toilet in the hope that the cool porcelain will do something to stop the constant night sweats. I've increased my weekly laundry by a good 30%—I usually go through four or five sets of pajamas and if I have managed to spend anytime in the bed, I often have to change the sheets about halfway through the night.

I had another appointment with Dr. L. last week, and I mentioned the side effects (vomiting, night sweats, etc.), but she didn't seem overly concerned. I figure it must be like this for everyone. As I have told myself over and over again in the last months, as long as it is working to fight this stupid thing—I can put up with my weekly snuggle-fest with the toilet.

Although she didn't seem overly interested in my reactions to the interferons, she was notably alarmed by my mobility, or lack there-of. When I attempted to perform the now familiar "walk of shame" down the hallway, I failed... miserably. As in I needed the wall to balance and even then, I managed to stumble. I didn't actually fall flat on my face in front of Dr. L. and the two nurses, but I came damn close. As I righted myself and attempted to continue towards the "finish line," I saw the look on each of their faces. There was shock and concern... but far worse, I detected pity, and that is the one thing that I have tried to avoid like the the plague. I do not want pity.

This isn't supposed to happen. I am young, vibrant, energetic, fit—I am not supposed to be clinging to the wall in some hospital hallway, pathetically trying to make it down a 50-foot "runway" with a team of medical experts looking on. I am supposed to be out running the hills of my neighborhood, kids and dogs in tow. I am supposed to be at the "prime of my life"—out showing the world how strong and fit I am. Instead, I had crumbled into one of two chairs positioned next to a built in platform that houses a computer screen and a bottle of Purell in the examination room, and waited for Dr. L.

That was last week, and as I wipe down the kitchen counter, having just finished the post-dinner clean up, my mind floats to the conversation that had followed my stumbling, near fall "stroll" down the hallway. Dr. L. thinks that I should get a "geriatric scooter" (well she said scooter, and I've now added the "geriatric" after searching the internet while waiting for the kids' mac 'n cheese to cook.) It is an old people thing. I look at it and immediately think of a bluehaired grandma chugging along, her front basket overflowing with all the things a grandma might need while out for a cruise. It may be politically incorrect for me to think this. I know that here are plenty of younger people with disabilities who use scooters as their means of mobility, but I am just not ready to accept that I am one of those "younger" people. I am not ready to accept that I am disabled.

But the truth is, I can't keep up. My walking, balance and mobility have all gone to shit over the past months. I finally broke down and bought a cane shortly after starting on my DMD. It took me over a month to build up the nerve to actually use it, out in public, where people could see (and judge). But after a pretty bad fall while at the kids' school for Spring concert night, I had heard one of the fathers mumble something to the effect of "drink much lately?", I decided that at least if I had a cane, and I stumbled or fell, people would at least know that there is something wrong with me—and that I am not just shit-faced drunk while attending my children's school performance.

But a scooter is on a whole different level—and as I wrap the kids up in their fluffy hooded towels and reach to drain the bath water from the tub, it hits me. One of the biggest fears I have about using a scooter is that people will be looking down on me. Not in the sense that they pity me (which, god forbid, I know I want to avoid at all costs) but physically. I will be seated, and they will be standing over me and I know that is something that I am not yet prepared to handle.

It's been a few weeks since Dr. L. mentioned the scooter and I have thought about it, but I just don't seem to be able to get over the idea of being beneath people. As I struggle down the hallway at my kids' school, making slow progress towards the classroom where I am volunteering this morning, my cane occasionally banging against the bank of lockers that line the halls, the most amazing thing happens. As I turn the corner, I see a head—seemingly float down the hallway in front of me. It's almost surreal looking, and I realize that one of the things that grabbed my attention was that it was a little person's head, but it was up high—like a tall little person gliding along.

It turns out, the head I saw belonged to a student that has physical disabilities. Depending on his condition and strength, he fluctuates between using arm crutches and a wheelchair. Until now, because now he is cruising around on a Segway—compliments of his amazing and creative parents. As I watch him maneuver the crowded hallway at passing time, and then later during recess out on the field playing tag with the other students, a lightbulb goes on. Maybe I could try a Segway. I have no idea how hard they are to ride, and truthfully, the idea of balancing on anything these days seems highly unlikely. But I have known this boy for years. I have seen how he struggles to walk and keep his balance and he is out there riding on it like it is second nature. If he can do it, maybe I can.

The minute I have the kids in bed, I begin my research. I quickly learn that Segways are not cheap, and picking up a "used" one on Craigslist doesn't seem likely. I read anything about Segways that I can find. I watch numerous YouTube videos (and become quite obsessed with one that has a chimpanzee riding on a Segway). But nothing I read or see answers the question of whether or not it would work for me. Whether me and my wonky-ass legs could even get on it, let alone cruise around on one. I learn that we have an actual Segway store here in Seattle and I jot down the number just before I close up my laptop, turn off the kitchen lights and head upstairs to bed.

I am feeling a bit giddy as I wait for 10 a.m. to roll around. That's when the Segway store opens. I had tried to stay focused this morning as I got the kids ready for school, but my mind kept going back to the videos I had watched last night. The people riding on them seemed to move with such ease, but more importantly, they seemed to be able to go on surfaces that I wouldn't have expected. Riding on trails and paths rather than just your standard sidewalk had grabbed my attention. If I can ride one, and it can go "off-road", then I would be able to keep up with the kids. I would be able to keep doing the things I used to do with them, like go to the beach or camping. Things that didn't seem to be "scooter-friendly."

When 10 a.m. finally comes, I call and I am put on the phone with Jack. When I explain that I have MS and that I am looking into getting a Segway as a means of mobility, he seems super intrigued and interested. He invites me to come in tomorrow morning to give one a test-ride and to see about renting one for a few days!

As I lay in bed, my mind keeps going back to my conversation with Jack. I realize that I might be setting myself up for disappointment, that I may not be able to even get on the damn thing. I know that I am putting all of my eggs in one basket with this idea, but my walking has really gone to shit. The idea that I might find something that will help me get around, while still on my own terms (still completely opposed to the idea of a scooter) is exciting. I feel like I am finally doing something to counteract this stupid disease and what it has done to my life.

Jack is a super great guy and we are quickly ensconced in a conversation about my diagnosis and my need for mobility assistance within minutes of arriving at the store. As I stand, leaning against my cane, I can feel my legs beginning to feel fatigued. This is what drives me crazy, I am just standing here and they are tired? WTF? What happened to miles and miles, hill after hill, pushing the mammoth double-jogger tireless through the streets of our neighborhood? How can my legs possibly be feeling done, after doing absolutely nothing?!?!

As Jack pulls a Segway out of the store and onto the sidewalk, I am growing concerned. My legs are really not happy that I have remained standing for the past thirty minutes, and they feel as if they are just about done. I've come to learn, when they are done, they are done. Game over. Maybe I shouldn't try and ride the Segway? Maybe I should come back another day when my legs are feeling better.

But then I realize that is the whole point. My legs are not going to feel better—or at least not all the time, and I need to find something that I can use specifically when my legs are done. So better to try it now and know. Jack pulls off a very impressive demo ride and then it is my turn. I prop my cane up against the side of the building and use his arm to steady myself as I climb onto the Segway. It shakes a bit, there is a bunch of vibrating, and it begins to rock back and forth. It is scary as shit, and I am thinking, "somebody get me off of this thing!!!" But Jack continues to hold onto my arm, as well as steadying the handlebar and the rocking subsides, and I am standing on the Segway. And I am taller than Jack… much taller. So far, so good.

I spend the next 10-15 minutes listening to Jack's instructions— learning how to make it go forward and backward. How to stop and how to turn. Then Jack announces that he thinks I've got it, and suggests that I take it for a spin around the block. Which scares the shit out of me. What if I fall? What if I crash into something??? Or worse, someone?? What if people just think I am a crazy nut? I am beginning to doubt this whole idea, when the voice in my head reminds me —it's either this or a scooter, and with that, I take off and zip around the corner of the building.

I am not going to lie. I absolutely love everything about it. I am standing tall, zipping in and out of the pedestrian traffic typical of a weekday mid-morning in Seattle. For the first time in a long time, I have no doubt that I will make it around the block and back to Jack. Given my wobbly legs and walking, there is no way that I could have managed this short journey without the aid of the Segway. I feel as if I have been given a small slice of my life back.

As I pull back up to the storefront, I am beaming. I can hardly contain my excitement—not only did it work for me but as I stand in front on Jack, still on the Segway, I realize that my legs don't hurt as much. As we are discussing the rental agreement, I am slowly rocking back and forth on the Segway. It's not moving, I am just rocking, and in doing so, I am stretching my legs and it seems to be helping, they don't feel as numb and fatigued. I'm not sure why this is, but I am willing to go with it.

I shake Jack's hand after we have loaded a rental Segway into Bessy. I make a note to myself that getting the Segway in and out of the car is going to be difficult. It is really heavy, and awkward to try and pick up. I wonder if my "man-child" Sam is strong enough to help me put it in and out of the car. He is into boxing these days, so maybe? But this seems trivial to me—having the Segway to ride even just out and about in our neighborhood is going to be life changing. I will be able to get out and do things and see people again. The small, enclosed circle of places I can go is about to expand and I am super excited to start the expansion.

My folks and I decide to take the kids up to the neighborhood pub that my husband owns. Walking up there to grab a bite to eat and allow the kids to spend some time with their dad is something that we do quite often. Or I should say did. For that past six months, if we have wanted to head up there, I would have to pack the kids into the car—just to drive the few short blocks because my legs wouldn't make the journey.

Tonight, as my kids run along the sidewalk, racing to keep up with me and my new set of wheels, I am filled with happiness and a sense of calm. I can do this—this whole "I have a chronic disease that is seriously fucking with me, but I am stronger and I will win" thing. So many times over the past year I have doubted myself. I have doubted that I can do this, that I can be strong enough to not only accept the changes to my life, but embrace them. I can't change that I have this stupid disease, but I can control how I go about living with it.

Riding along on my rented Segway, I run into neighbors that I haven't seen in months. I am surprised to see that a house that I have walked by for years has been torn down. As I glide along, I look up and notice the cherry trees are beginning to blossom. These are the things that I have been missing being confined to the house and the driver's seat of Bessy. These are the things that I am thankful to have back in my life at the moment.

The minute I get home, I leave a message for Segway Jack—telling him I want to order one. I have no idea how I am going to swing this financially—because they are not cheap, and Jack had explained to me that insurance would not cover the cost of the purchase, even if I am using it as my "means of mobility." But even if I have to go pimp myself out on some street corner (I am sure I would stand out on the Segway), I need to get one.

As I hang up the phone, my father walks into the kitchen, and I put to words what I have been thinking.

"Dad, I need one."

"Then we will get you one."

This is why I love my parents. This is why I know that I will be OK and that I will continue to find ways around the bullshit that Multiple Sclerosis brings into my life.

My very own Segway arrives two weeks later and the kids name it Mojo. In no time flat, I become a skilled and expert Segway operator. I love the freedom it has brought back into my life. I love that I am able to be a chaperone at sleepover camp and that thanks to Mojo, my team wins Capture the Flag all three nights. No one could come close to catching me. Granted, the kids on the losing team felt that this was unfair, but I explain to them that people with disabilities need special accommodations, and my special accommodation was that I could go super fast, kind of like a super power.

I slowly grow used to the chronic looks and comments that Mojo and I get. I often feel uncomfortable, because I am no longer anonymous, and I fear that people will think that I am trying to draw attention to myself. But then I remember that I am doing simple tasks like getting milk and eggs at the grocery store, or taking my kids to the park. Things that I would not be able to do if it weren't for Mojo, and I tell myself to stop worrying about what other people say or think.

It's Monday morning, school is done for the year and the kids and I have the whole summer ahead of us. Places to go, things to see... but at the moment, we are in Costco. Mojo and I glide along next the cart that seems to dwarf my growing children. I have always loved coming here with them, oftentimes making a game of the kids finding the products and things we need. These days, I have figured out that having them with me is a necessity. If not for them, I would have no one to push the enormous cart. Although my Segway riding skills are pretty fierce these days—pushing a cart while riding it is not a skill I have mastered. I have just turned the corner into the aisle where the milk and eggs are located, when a woman lets out an audible yelp. I try and make eye contact, but she is too busy mumbling something to her male companion. As I roll past her, the kids are close behind me. I hear the woman say, "no fair, I want one." Followed by, "Really? Because my mom wants legs that work, want to trade?"

The waterworks hit immediately. As I spin to face my child that has just left me absolutely speechless, I know that I should be reprimanding him for talking back to an adult. That's what the old me would have done. The mom I was before being diagnosed with MS. For as much time and energy I expend towards not letting this disease change me, it obviously is changing me. It is making me see what is really important in life. What really matters. It is teaching me what I should teach my kids. What values and manners really matter. I think about what I should say. What is the right thing to say in a moment like this? Is it finally time for me to tell him that people can be assholes, but that he should learn to ignore them?

I roll right up, into the woman's personal space, look down at her and simply say, "He's right, you know." I, then, perform a perfect pivot towards the kids with a huge ass smile on my face and say, "who wants a hot dog and a smoothie?"

Chapter Twelve

Tysabri: The Elephant In the Room

"Opening up to people, letting your guard down and asking for help is NOT a sign of weakness. It is a sign that you are a badass doing what is necessary to move forward and find happiness."

It's been a year since I started sticking a needle in my thigh once a week. It's been six months since my last MRI. I'm winding through the Arboretum, heading to the lab that houses the enormous magnetic tube where I will be spending the next few hours. It's not yet 6 a.m., and already it is obvious that it is going to be a cold, wet Sunday. I guess spending it in a tube isn't that bad. What does suck is that once again, I am heading in for a medical procedure, alone.

When I think about how much my life has changed, I feel a deep sense of loneliness. I have always been a strong, independent person. I have always done things on my own. I have friends, great people that I spend time with, but not many with whom I am close. Over the past eighteen months, I have been driven by the need to show the world how strong I am, how well I am handling all this shit—but in doing so, I have managed to construct a fortress around my thoughts and feelings. I spend so much time telling everyone that I am "good," "great," or "fine" that I can't imagine actually opening up and telling anyone how all of this is really affecting me.

I think of my husband, still snuggled under the down comforter in our bed, more than likely unaware that I have left, that I am no longer in bed or even in the house. I had told him about the MRI when I scheduled it last week. I had hoped that maybe he would at least offer to accompany me since I had shipped all three kids off to a friend's house for a sleepover (knowing that I would be up and gone so early in the morning). Instead, when he asked last night where the kids were and I reminded him of the appointment, his response was, "Great! That means I can sleep in!"

I'm not sure my marriage is going to make it. I'm not sure I can take the sadness of being married to someone who doesn't seem to want to be with me, doesn't seem to like me. I know that the stress and strain that stems from a diagnosis like Multiple Sclerosis can take its toll on a marriage. I know that my husband has had to come to terms with all these changes and how they affect his life. I know that this disease affects all of us. But I don't want to be alone. I don't want to be unhappy. I am beginning to realize that part of thinking about myself and trying to take care of me for once is coming to the realization that settling for a marriage that leaves me feeling empty and sad might be more detrimental to my health than this stupid disease.

Monday morning, as I pull to the curb to drop the kids off, my phone rings. I see that it is Dr. L.'s office. She has already had a chance to review the result of yesterday's MRI and she would like to see me, ASAP. This can't be good. I make an appointment for tomorrow morning and head off to hit the gym and run errands before school lets out.

Sitting in her office, waiting for her to knock on the door and enter, I am worried about the MRI. What had she seen that required me to come in "as soon as possible?" Again, thoughts spring up in my mind. Maybe it isn't MS after all, maybe I do have that tumor that I had once imagined. Maybe it's something different all together? Maybe they were completely wrong, and this is all going to go away—all the symptoms and discomfort will just stop and I will have my life back? Maybe. There always seems to be that flicker of hope.

Maybe they got it all wrong and it is all going to go away and I can be "just me" again!

I'm not sure why I keep doing this to myself. Thinking that maybe someone got it wrong. I guess it's because I really still can't believe that I have Multiple Sclerosis (or any disease for that matter.) It wasn't in my plans. It's not something that I had dreamed of—imagining as a small child, what it would be like to live with a chronic disease. Kids don't think about shit like that. Although maybe my kids will now, now that their mom has one and has become disabled.

Thinking of that word brings a smile to my face, as I remember a conversation I had with Sam the other day. He had overheard me on the phone. I had called the Washington State Department of Motor Vehicles. I was inquiring about getting a disability placard. At some point in the conversation, I apparently had said, "I am disabled." When I hung up the phone, I had been surprised to find Sam standing right behind me, with his hands on his hips and a snarl on his face.

"Mom! You are not disabled!!!"

"Oh, honey, it's just the term that they use to indicate that I need a little special attention."

"No, mom! You are not disabled! You are able to do anything you want! You just do it with a handicap. Like when dad plays golf."

Seeing how my kids have dealt with my diagnosis, watching them just roll with whatever new thing that happens, makes me swell with pride. They are great little people, and they are actually becoming better little people because of this stupid disease. They are learning to have empathy. To sympathize with others and find the reasons to laugh and smile about all the stupid shit the disease doles out.

Dr. L. enters and gets right down to business. Apparently the MRI shows "significant progression" and she is suggesting that I stop taking

Avonex, and move on to the next option, called Tysabri. Hearing that the scans had revealed that the Avonex didn't seem to be doing jack shit (other than making me sick for 12-15 hours every week) made it super easy for me to agree to changing to a new therapy (another term that refers to the disease modifying drugs).

Again, there is a process for getting approval, both from the insurance company and the pharmaceutical company. Dr. L. explains that it has been approved by the FDA—despite running into a few "hurdles" with something called PML (Progressive multifocalleukoencephalopathy—which is a rare disease of the brain). A screening process and safety measures have been put in place to ensure that patients at risk for PML will not receive the drug. It is one more thing for me to worry about, but I trust Dr. L. and if she is recommending it, then I am in.

I want to continue to fight against this disease and if I failed at giving myself shots, why not try letting someone else give them to me? My new therapy will involve visiting the infusion center every twenty-eight days for approximately four hours. I, of course, begin planning out my days when I will be getting the medicine, calculating when I can make it into the center in between drop-offs and pick-ups. After all, above all else, I need to keep being mom. It's what I do and it is what I love.

A few weeks have passed since my visit with Dr. L. and I got a call yesterday from a nurse in the infusion center, wanting to set up my first dose. So after dropping the kids off at a friend's house (it's a conference day at their school), I head to the hospital. I visit with a few of the nurses before I check into the infusion center, and have a seat in one of the large, padded seats. I do notice that they are much nicer than the ones at the center where I got my steroids and am happy to discover that they are also much more comfortable. Given that this is where I will be spending the next four plus hours, my ass and legs are grateful for this upgrade in seating assignments.

The procedure goes very smoothly. Nurse Tom is a wizard at putting the line in. I hardly even notice and in no time, the drug is pumping through my veins. As I lean back and try to rest, I imagine a bunch of knights mounted on horseback charging with their swords, arrows and axes flung forward—ready to beat the shit out of this stupid disease. I know that it sounds like a child's dream or fantasy about wiping out the disease. I know that medically it isn't what is happening within the walls of my body, but it helps to visualize it this way. It makes me feel optimistic that maybe this is the thing that my body needs to slow down the progression of the disease.

That night, as I am tucking the kids into bed, I share this funny image with them. I describe all the little knights, mounted and in line, ready for the call to begin the attack. They love the idea of these tiny men charging in to fight the disease and we spend almost an hour describing the battles, talking about what the MS Monster looks like—and even drawing some pictures of what they think it looks like inside my body. As I climb into bed, I am thinking about the knights and their battle, and I hope that they are good warriors and that they will claim victory over the monster that is now a constant companion in our lives.

Although I have been warned that it can take up to six months to notice improvements, I have been feeling so much better over the past twenty-eight days. I have more energy, less of the constant and all consuming fatigue and even a little bit less numbness and pain in my feet and legs. I don't know that I have seen any improvement in my balance or walking—but to have any positive changes is a relief. I was beginning to think that nothing was going to help. Nothing was going to stop the stupid monster from taking over my life.

When I arrive to the infusion center, I am in high spirits. I chat with Tom as he puts the line in and then wait for the medicine to arrive from the pharmacy upstairs. I notice a man sitting in the chair next to mine. I surprise myself with my initial reaction, "he doesn't look sick." Holy shit!—did I just really think that? After all, I am living proof that looks can be deceiving. I remind myself that there are thousands of other people out there—living with diseases and symptoms that are not visible to the outside world. Up until this point, I have been very self-centered or self-focused about this disease. I have spent time and energy learning about it, living with it because I have it. I haven't really thought about other people having it. I have thought about other people living with it.

I find myself borderline stalking the man. I now want to know his story. I want to know what disease he has. Does he has MS like me? Maybe he can be my very first MS BFF!

Just after Tom returns to hook up the bag of drugs to my IV line, a woman walks into the room and heads straight towards me. Well actually towards my new "MS BFF" that I haven't yet met. His eyes are closed, and he doesn't see her approaching, and there is such a kind, caring, loving look on her face as she gently nudges his knee and holds out a Starbucks cup towards him. When his eyes open, the look of sheer joy and raw happiness that takes his face hostage, leaves me breathless, and the waterworks threaten to make an appearance. I have no idea why watching a woman (not necessarily even a spouse) delivering coffee to someone in the middle of an infusion room has me bordering on being a mess, but I am pretty sure it is because I would really love to have someone to bring me a cup of coffee. I would really love to open my eyes to discover that someone has come to visit me.

As I continue to eavesdrop on my neighbor, my arm begins to itch. At first, I am too busy listening for any scrap of information about my new MS BFF and his coffee delivering companion, but eventually, both my arms are itching, and scratching them through my heavy sweater isn't providing much relief. As I pull the sweater over my head, using caution to not disturb the needle in my arm I am shocked and alarmed to discover that both my arms are covered in hives. Big, red, itchy lumps all over my arms.

I immediately reach for the button to summon the nurse. As I stand next to my chair, trying to not scratch at my arms but miserably failing, my new MS BFF looks over at me and says, "Oh that can't be good. You OK?" See? Someone cares about me! This man that I don't know, that I have never met, that I know nothing about is concerned for my wellbeing! See? I matter to someone! Being alone sucks!

Nurse Tom arrives and the look of alarm on his face does nothing to squelch the mounting fear that has crept into my mind. Holy shit! What is happening? Is this PML? Am I dying?!? I am really not sure how much more of this "being sick" stuff I can put up with. I am just about ready to throw in the towel. Give up and just let the stupid monster win.

It turns out, I am having an allergic reaction to the medication. Nurse Tom assures me that although it is not common, that it is nothing to be worried about. He explains that it does occasionally happen to patients during their first few infusions and that with the aid of hydrocortisone and Benadryl, they can control the hives and safely continue administering the drugs into my body. He says all of this, while pushing both in my IV line. By the time he has finished explaining and checking my blood pressure, the itching has subsided and I no longer feel the urge to rip my arms off.

We are able to continue the infusion after about thirty minutes and by the time the IV bag is empty, there is no sign of the hives that had taken over my arms. My arms are back to feeling "normal" and don't itch, even when I put my heavy wool sweater back on. As Nurse Tom pulls the needle out of my arm and wraps a bit of gauze around my forearm to ward off the few drops of blood that always seem to make their way out of the injection site before clotting up, he mentions that Dr. L. wants to see me.

Oh shit—why does this feel like I am being called down to the principal's office? Why do I feel as if I have failed again? I've been feeling better. I swear that I have already begun to notice improvements. Now what?

Dr. L. arrives at the side of my chair a few minutes later. I'm pretty sure that I see pity flash across her face, but it is fleeting, and I'm not completely certain it was even there. After all, I am a bit upset. I don't want to have failed yet another DMD. She repeats all the same stuff Nurse Tom had shared, about a small percentage of patients having an allergic reaction but I am not focused on her words. I am feeling overwhelmed with frustration. Why is this not working? Why does my body continue to fuck with me, when I am trying to do the right thing? I am trying so hard to be a fighter!

Dr. L. assures me that the fact that I responded so well to the anti-allergy medications is a good sign. She says that it means that I can continue on the Tysabri and explains that they will take measures to try and ensure that I don't get hives again. They will put the Benadryl and the hydrocortisone into my bloodstream thirty minutes before they start the infusion. She assures me that this has worked for other patients and she expresses that she is hopeful that this solution will work for me.

As I pack up my bag, and reach to put my coat and scarf on, I notice that my MS BFF is still here and that both he and his female sidekick have been listening to every word that Dr. L. said. As I walk out, I have to laugh to myself thinking, "who is the stalker now?" It seems that I always end up with the interesting story.

The next twenty-eight days fly by as the kids and I are busy enjoying the final days of summer and gearing up for the start of school. I haven't thought much about what happened or about what might happen. I have thought a lot about how I have been feeling—because I have definitely noticed improvements; in the pain, in the fatigue and foggy brain, and even with the walking. I swear my balance has improved, although I still need either the cane or Mojo with me at all times. I am quickly learning that small improvements mean a whole lot when it comes to this disease.

When I check into the infusion center, I'm told that Nurse Tom is on vacation and that Rachel will be helping me. It's a rough go with trying to get the line into my arm. Although I mention that my veins tend to roll, she seems gung-ho when she sees my veins. Apparently they look nice today, but I am living proof that looks can be deceiving. Four failed attempts and quite a bit of pain as she rooted around trying to get into a vein, and she had the line in. For the next thirty minutes, the Benadryl and hydrocortisone flow into my body—I'm now imagining that they are the knights entering into a battle against the drug that is supposed to be helping me get better. It all strikes me as a bit backwards, but I still feel strongly that I need to do this to have a chance against the monster.

Once the last drops of the allergy medications have entered into my bloodstream, I am hooked up to the bag containing the DMD. About five minutes into the infusion, my head begins to feel funny, like I am suddenly drunk. I start having trouble getting enough air into my lungs. It feels like a giant elephant has plopped down on my chest and the only thing I want to do is rip the IV line out of my arm. As I reach out to hit the buzzer to get Rachel's attention, I start sweating and shaking. By the time she reaches my chair, I have vomited down my front.

I'm pretty sure this is not how it is supposed to go.

As Rachel is pushing more Benadryl and hydrocortisone into the line another nurse is leaning over me, loosening my shirt and wiping my face with a damp cloth. I smell vomit. I swear I can feel the drug running through my bloodstream. I imagine that this must be what it feels like to be a drug user that shoots up with some bad mix of stuff. Knowing it is now in my body, with no available exits. It's in there and it is fucking with me and there is nothing I can do about it!

At some point a screen is pulled around my chair, my limp, vomit covered body hidden from the others in the infusion center. I wonder if my MS BFF is out there, worrying about me. Probably not.

As I begin to come out of it and stabilize, I realize that there is another person in my little cocoon. She introduces herself as Dr. W. and explains that Dr. L. is out of the office for the day but that she is one of the other MS doctors here at the clinic. She seems kind, and seems genuinely concerned about me, but I can't help but think, "I want my own doctor! I want Dr. L., who knows me, knows that I don't want pity, knows that I have to get my kids, knows that I have a husband who has never been to a single appointment." She knows my life and Dr. W. doesn't and it sucks because I feel alone and overcome with sadness.

As she is being brought up to speed on my medical background, and the events that just occurred, another person enters my coccoon. It's getting pretty crowded in here and I am beginning to feel a panic attack coming on. It is the other mom that works with Dr. L. Someone has gone and found her and she is now asking me how she can get ahold of my husband.

My husband. Where is my husband? How can they get ahold of him. All simple questions and none of which I have an answer for. I don't know where he is and it's not because my mind is unclear from what just happened. I honestly don't know where he is. I know that he mentioned that he was going on a golfing trip. I had heard the garage door early this morning and as I rolled over to try and get a few more minutes of sleep, I remember thinking he must have left an itinerary. But later on, as I got the kids fed and out the door for school, I realized that there was no itinerary, no note, no nothing. I have no idea where he went, or how long he is going to be gone.

I say none of this to the other mom. I give her his phone number and say, "he doesn't answer his phone very often."

It's been about four hours since my body freaked out and decided to scare the shit out of me. Since then, I have learned that I had been in what they call anaphylactic shock—that my reaction to the drug was much more severe than anyone had anticipated. The other mom has informed me that she has left "several" messages for my husband, but has not heard back from him. I am not surprised. This makes me sad.

Not being able to track him down, I call a friend and arrange for her to pick the kids up from school. It kills me to be doing this, to allow the stupid disease to win this one, but given the fact that my clothes are coated in vomit, and it doesn't seem like they are going to let me out of here anytime soon, I don't really have other options. I can't depend on my husband to help me out, because I don't know where he is, so I will rely on the people that have been there, and have offered up their support. I am going to rely on my friends and ask for help. I don't really have a choice.

Chapter Thirteen

Divorce—A Fork in the Road

"Don't be afraid. Things may get worse before they get better but I have confidence in you. You are a one strong person and you are going to be OK."

It's been four days since "it" happened. That is what I am calling it. Just "it." Because I am not really sure what else to call it. A severe reaction for sure. But that doesn't really seem to convey all that happened; all that I've lived through and all the emotions that I have experienced since that day. When I think about it, it scares the shit out of me. To think that I could go from everything being just fine—happy-go-lucky me, chilling and chit chatting with the nurses and staff, to not being able to get enough air in my lungs, shaking violently and vomiting on myself in just a few short minutes is mind blowing.

In the past four days, I have asked myself, "how did I get here?" more times than I can count. It's not really about the disease, I don't really care "how" I got it, or even "why." This is about how I am married to someone that is effectively a complete stranger. When I got home from the hospital that day, I had plopped the kids in front of the TV and tried to call him. It went straight to voicemail. I knew for a fact that the other mom that works for Dr. L. had left messages, that she had explained that it was a medical emergency and yet he didn't answer. I left a brief message giving a rundown of what had happened and then snuggled up with the kids on the couch and called to have pizza delivered. He called at 10 p.m.—I let his call go to voicemail.

Since then, we have barely spoken about "it." He knows that I had some "sort of a reaction" to a medicine, but that is about it. Not because I don't want to share, but because he doesn't ask.

Dr. L. called this morning. Apparently I have developed "antibody-positivity" to the drug. I have to be honest and admit I didn't understand much of what she said, but the gist I got was that my body would continue to fight the drug until the end, as in my end. I guess there are knights with swords, arrows and axes in a battle within my body as I had visualized but apparently they are fighting the medicine and not the monster!

I spend the day sitting on a bench on the edge of the lake. I don't know that I have ever been here by myself. It's where I go with the kids. Where I take the dogs to cool off. Where I meet other moms to hang out while the kids go for a swim. But never by myself. But today, I just need to be by myself. I need to think about what it is that I want from my life now that I am living with this incurable disease.

As I throw stale bread at the ducks, I mull over everything that has happened since receiving my diagnosis. I think back to hearing the "Poker Playing" doctor say the words and truthfully, there was actually a part of me that was hopeful. I remember thinking that perhaps this was the life event that would shake things up in my marriage and then dump us back down on an even and new playing field. Remembering those thoughts, and then comparing them to what the reality has been leaves me with a sad smile pasted on my face.

As a cold breeze sweeps in from off the lake, I shudder—more out of sadness and disappointment than from feeling chilled by the damp air that is forever present here in the Pacific Northwest. It strikes me as a bit ironic, that I chose to get married and I can't seem to make it work. I had no choice in getting a chronic disease and I seem to be just rolling with it and accepting the changes as they come.

As I head towards the school to pick up the kids, I make a promise to myself. I am going to ask my husband for a divorce. As hard as I have tried to keep things "normal" to ensure that things are the "same" and that the disease isn't winning—I have come to realize that "same" isn't good enough. It has taken me getting this disease, it has taken all that I have been through over the past few years to admit that I deserve better, that I deserve to be happy. Being diagnosed with this disease has given me the strength to want to pull the plug and leave the unhappiness behind. I love being a mom and I have great friends and family but I have known for years that there should be more to a marriage than just "coexisting" under one roof. I have not felt love, friendship or intimacy in our relationship for years and I now feel as if I need those things more than ever.

I realize that deciding to end my marriage when I am a living with a chronic illness that fucks with me every day, and that might leave me disabled and unable to care for myself might sound crazy. But I have recently come to the realization that I am already going through all of it alone and I would rather just know that I need to rely on myself rather than always hoping that maybe something will change and maybe today will be the day that he comes to visit and brings me that cup of coffee.

Getting this disease has made me know that I am strong enough and brave enough to believe in myself and it has made me want to push for something more. It has made me want to pull my big girl panties up and not only survive whatever shit the disease throws as me, but find the reasons to laugh and smile through it all.

Physically, my life has changed drastically in a short period of time. I went from running 6-8 miles six days a week to needing to use a cane or my Segway to get to the bus stop at the end of the block. I rely on wall-walking to get around in the house and have had more than one tumble down the stairs as I try desperately to continue what I have always done. From day one, when my "Poker Playing" doctor told me that this isn't an "oh fuck" moment, I have tried my best to not let the disease or its symptoms get the best of me. I worked my ass off to stay physically strong.

But the biggest change to my life has been an emotional one. Prior to my diagnosis, I had succumbed to the idea that my story was already written; that a life of living with someone that was more like a room-mate than a partner and oftentimes feeling like a single parent was just the way that my life would be. But getting this disease, living with MS, has shown me that the unexpected can certainly happen.

Life has changed and I am trying with all my might to leave that old life and person behind and finally be true to myself and who I want to be. Even if I have an incurable disease and it often seems to have the last word, I am going to give happiness a shot.

Meg Lewellyn, a physically fit mother of three, was diagnosed with Multiple Sclerosis in 2007. Along with the weighty health obstacle of being diagnosed with this often debilitating neurological condition, her marriage was tested to its very limits and ended in divorce in 2011. Following her diagnosis, she tried countless medications to slow the progression of the disease and minimize its daily effects on her life.

After nearly hitting rock bottom with diminished quality of life and immense pain, she decided to question everything that she had been raised to believe and tried cannabis and cannabidol (CBD) to manage her chronic pain and MS symptoms. That was two years ago — currently, she is off of all prescription drugs and medications and is able to manage her symptoms naturally through diet, exercise and medical marijuana.

In 2018, Meg married husband 2.0 — her greatest supporter and advocate. They live in Renton, Washington with their two dogs, her youngest son and Doug — the name of their first cannabis plant. Outside of the labels of Cannabis Advocate, Lifestyle Blogger and MSer, Meg is an avid angler and hiker. They can often be found out on their fishing boat named 'Blood & Bong Water', hiking in the vast mountain ranges of the Pacific Northwest and attending cannabis expos and events to share her story and educate people about a plant that once scared the hell out of her.

Through the years, Meg has continued to write about her experiences on her blog BBHwithMS.com. Follow Meg and her husband on their MMJ adventures as they continue to discover the hacks that allow her to keep kicking MS's ass — not allowing it to define who she is or what she is capable of.

Made in the USA
Columbia, SC
03 November 2018